HANNU MÄKELÄ

MR. BOO

HANNU MÄKELÄ

MR. BOO

Drawings by
Hannu Mäkelä

Translated by
Anselm Hollo

ASPASIA BOOKS
BEAVERTON ONTARIO CANADA

ASPASIA CHILDREN'S BOOKS

Mr Boo
ISSN 1702-9597; ISBN 0-9689054-8-X
Published in 2002 by
Aspasia Books
R.R.1, Beaverton, Ontario L0K 1A0 Canada
aspasia@aspasiabooks.com
www.aspasiabooks.com

Translated from the Finnish original *Herra Huu* by Hannu Mäkelä
First published in 1973 by Otava (Helsinki, Finland)
Drawings by Hannu Mäkelä

Aspasia Children's Books

© Hannu Mäkelä (Finnish original)
© Anselm Hollo (English translation)
© Aspasia Books (English language edition)

Cover design by Martin Best of My6productions from
drawings by Hannu Mäkelä.

*Aspasia Books gratefully acknowledges the assistance of the Finnish
Literature Information Center*

Aspasia Children's Books series editor Börje Vähämäki.

Printed and bound in Canada by University of Toronto Press

National Library of Canada Cataloguing in Publication

Mäkelä, Hannu
    **Mr. Boo / Hannu Mäkelä ; drawings by Hannu Mäkelä ; translated
by Anselm Hollo.**

(Aspasia children's books)
Translation of: Herra Huu.
ISBN 0-9689054-8-X

    I. Hollo, Anselm II. Title. III. Series.

PZ7.M285Mi 2002   **j894'.54133**   **C2002-904553-3**

Mr. Boo Goes to Work

Mr. Boo opened his eyes but closed them again when he noticed the sun was shining. He wrapped himself more tightly in his blanket. He didn't have to worry about school or playschool or a new working day. He slept in the daytime and got up whenever he felt like it.

Now he was asleep again. And he was snoring. "RAWR RAWR RAWR," he said, sounding like an engine that won't start. Then, suddenly, Mr. Boo got up, looked outside and saw that it was already getting quite dark. That meant he had to get up, no matter how tired he was.

Mr. Boo worked nights. He'd done so ever since his Dad had suddenly taken off and left him with his grandfather. Grandpa had taught him to read and do magic and live the way he himself did. Mr. Boo had become used to it.

A creaking door ...
A squeaking floor ...
The flash of a knife ...
Who is it, who?
None other than
tough little Mr. Boo.

A twig snaps in the woods — it's Mr. Boo. Something moves under your bed — it's Mr. Boo. And at night, when something rustles and bustles around the kitchen, it is that same wild Mr. Boo in his black cloak.

Mr. Boo didn't like to work. He slept whenever he could. But there were times he just couldn't fall asleep, no matter how hard he tried. He had to drag himself out of bed and get going, muttering under his breath. It was cold, wet, and gloomy. Sure, he did not have to punch a time clock — but on the other hand, he didn't have any insurance, no place to warm up in, no regular income, no compensation for odd working hours. No pension for him when he got old. All he could call his own was a little cottage, and that would disappear soon enough, he thought gloomily. It would be displaced by the big new stone buildings going up in the city.

Now he was resolutely marching along, even though he had the flu again. Mr. Boo couldn't see a doctor. Doctors were afraid of him. They told him he didn't exist. Doctors did not write prescriptions or medical excuse notes for Mr. Boo. On the other hand, they didn't charge him anything, either.

The road was wet and long and Mr. Boo couldn't stop sneezing. Then he heard a rustling sound ahead of him. He hid behind a rock.

The steps approached. Someone was coming ... Now!

With a roar Mr. Boo jumped out from behind the rock. But it wasn't really a roar because his throat was so sore that he could hardly make a noise. It was so sore that it amazed Mr. Boo to think that he'd been able to eat something not too long ago. And the tall man walked past Mr. Boo, thinking about cream cakes. The tall man didn't even notice him.

Well, that was a fiasco, thought Mr. Boo. Then he sneezed again. There was a light on in a nearby house. In the yard stood an apple tree with dark, somber branches. That's where I'll go, decided Mr. Boo, and climbed up into the apple tree.

Watch out for weak branches, Mr. Boo! Crash. And Mr. Boo lay on the ground.

One side of his chest felt sore, he'd scraped skin off an index finger, and his flu was getting worse. Aspirin is not working, thought Mr. Boo. He started dragging himself back home. He kicked a rock that lay in the road and hurt his toe. The last bat of autumn floated over his head like a kite, scaring him. An automobile roared past and spattered Mr. Boo with slush. People were yelling in a nearby house, celebrating someone's birthday. Mr. Boo shuddered.

A faint light shone from under the dark autumn trees: it was a small cottage. Perhaps it belongs to people as small as I am, thought Mr. Boo. The thought cheered him up a little. Perhaps they'll be afraid of me. Quietly he snuck up to the wall of the cottage and peeked through a window.

In a little room, a little girl lay in a little bed. She was reading a little book. This is my chance, Mr. Boo decided. He opened the window from the outside — all Mr. Boos know that trick — and slid down to the floor without a sound.

The little girl didn't suspect or notice anything. Her name was Rimma, and she had just celebrated her sixth birthday. She had just started learning to read, as well, but she hadn't brushed her teeth before going to bed. She shared the cottage with her old grandma and a cat, and the cat had gone off on its rounds and had forgotten to remind Rimma to brush her teeth. Grandma was sipping coffee in the kitchen and thinking about things that had happened to her when she was young, the way all grandmothers do in all the kitchens of small Finnish cottages. Rimma was spelling out words in her book. It was called True Ghost Stories.

ONCE UP-ON A TIME THERE WAS A GHOST THAT WOULD HOWL HORR-IB-LY.

"AAAAAAAARGHHHH," Mr. Boo shouted and charged into the middle of the floor, raising his arms and showing his teeth. But all that emerged from his throat was a little hiss. A puddle of water slid off his coat onto the floor. He sneezed again. The little girl tossed the book aside and looked at Mr. Boo, genuinely surprised. .

"Who are you?"

Mr. Boo croaked:

"I am the wild and scary Mr. Boo!
No one does worse things than I can do!
I catch little children,
I throw them in a pot
and boil them for dinner!
It sure hits the spot!"

Then he sneezed again. The girl smiled at Mr. Boo.

"I was just trying to read about ghosts. But it's easier when you really get to see one. Scare me, please!"

Mr. Boo tried. He roared like a lion, hissed like a tiger, chattered like a baboon, tore the wallpaper to shreds, made faces, and appeared all over the place, causing a lot of commotion.

The girl laughed. "I haven't had this much fun for a long time," she said.

"I'm cold," Mr. Boo muttered. He was tired and disappointed and wanted to go home. "I think I'll be on my way now," he said and sidled over to the window.

"Promise to come back," the girl shouted, waving goodbye. "My name is Rimma."

"We'll see," Mr. Boo said cautiously and slipped outside. He didn't know what to think. He hurried down the road. An automobile swooshed by and Mr. Boo got so scared his heart started pounding. This is no way to live. I have a weak heart, and if I die, no one will come to my funeral. Mr. Boo felt weepy.

It was warm in his cottage. Water was steaming in a pot on the stove. Mr. Boo made some tea with honey and heated up some currant juice, dried his clothes, and went to bed. But sleep wouldn't come. I better read something, Mr. Boo thought and picked a book off the floor. It was called "1001 Magical and Sinister Ways to Frighten People." That didn't work either. The words ran away from his eyes, the letters turned into wriggly lines of ants and mounds of aphids. I've become old, Mr. Boo thought and felt depressed. Then some awful howling outside scared him again. But it was just a stray dog.

After a while Mr. Boo calmed down and fell asleep. The logs in the stove began to glow and darken. The whole cottage wrapped itself in a warm blanket and slept.

Mr. Boo and the Sick Tree

In the morning Mr. Boo woke up feeling quite refreshed. Is it day? he wondered. I haven't been awake in the daytime for quite a while. He went to the window and looked out. A yellow leaf floated past the window. Mr. Boo was appalled.

What was this? The tree must be sick. It worried him. I must help it, thought Mr. Boo. He went through his chest of drawers and picked out band-aids, a needle, some thread, a pair of scissors, and some medicine.

Outside, everything looked quite different from the way it looked at night. For one thing, it was incredibly bright out there. The yellow leaf had landed on the thorn of a rose. It wasn't the only one. There were more yellow and brown leaves under the apple tree.

Mr. Boo fetched a ladder, leaned it against the tree, and climbed it cautiously. He applied band-aids, sewed and sewed, until all the leaves were back on their twigs and branches again. That done, he poured some cough medicine on the ground by the roots of the tree and went back in.

He sat down on the edge of his bed and pondered things. He decided to think about all the nice things that had happened to him. For a long while he sat there very quietly, but in the end he had to admit to himself he just couldn't remember any such things. Maybe they didn't exist. The room looked unreal to him, and he closed his eyes, so it would be dark. Maybe it was possible to get used to the light if one tried really hard, he thought. Then he fell asleep.

That night, he had a long vivid dream in which a long line of sharp objects advanced straight at him. After a while, he woke up. At last, the dark grew softer, became gray, then light. Mr. Boo couldn't go back to sleep, and when morning came, he got up and started moving around his room.

Mr. Boo looked outside. The tree was there, next to the window, as it had always been. But, goodness! Once again, it had dropped a lot of leaves. The ground was covered with them. That tree must be seriously ill, thought Mr. Boo. I have to help it. He gathered up band-aids, needle, thread, and medicine, and went outside to put up the ladder again.

All day, Mr. Boo sewed, put on band-aids, medicated the leaves back onto the tree. In the evening, he was so tired he fell asleep without having time to think about anything at all.

In the morning, Mr. Boo woke up again. There must be something wrong with me, he thought. Never before have I woken up so many times when it's light outside. He pulled the blanket over himself and decided to stay in bed all day. Maybe sleep would surprise him and bring back his very own dark nights. Then he remembered the tree.

Cautiously, Mr. Boo turned his head toward the window and peeked, then quickly turned his head back again. That can't be my tree. There are hardly any leaves on it.

Mr. Boo turned back, looked at the window again. The tree was there, and it stayed there, and it was practically leafless. The only leaves left were the ones Mr. Boo had sewn and attached with band-aids. This is terrible, thought Mr. Boo, that tree will die soon. With a sigh, he took out the needle, the scissors, the thread and the medicine and went outside. He spent the whole day sewing, putting on band-aids, fixing and medicating. It was quite dark before he had managed to attach all the leaves to the branches. When he got to his bed he fell on it like a pinetree cut down by a chainsaw and slept like a log until morning.

When he woke up and glanced outside he saw that all the leaves were still firmly attached to the tree. Mr. Boo felt proud. I've nursed the tree back to health, he thought. I don't need to get up today. And he turned around and slept until the evening.

The leaves stayed on Mr. Boo's tree all winter. Mr. Boo had a prettier and healthier apple tree than anybody else. All the leaves had fallen off the other trees and turned into a brownish mess on the ground. I'll be the only one who gets some winter apples, thought Mr. Boo and felt sorry for the other people. They could learn a lot from me, he thought.

Mr. Boo Goes Fishing

Mr. Boo had heard people say that it was fall. In the fall, people went fishing! He went to his closet to get — what? He stopped to think. Then he remembered. What you needed was a fishing rod, and a hook, and a bob, and what else? That's right, a line. Mr. Boo rummaged in his closet.

Finally he was ready. Mr. Boo gulped down a cup of properly brewed Earl Grey tea, the only kind he liked, and clumped and clattered to the door. The fishing rod was heavy. I bet I'll catch some big fish with this, thought Mr. Boo. People weren't supposed to see him, so he walked down the shady side of the road. He passed the cottage in which the girl Rimma lived with her grandma. He looked at it cautiously. One of these nights I'll go there and scare her to death, he thought grimly and hurried on.

It was cold out on the road. Mr. Boo's ears were cold and the fishing rod got heavier and heavier. Why am I doing this? he asked himself. I'll go into the woods, perhaps it is warmer there. But, oh no: something shiny crunched under his feet. What is this? Mr. Boo wondered. Glass, in my woods? Someone must have smashed a lot of windows. Well, that's because the city is getting closer and closer to these parts, he thought. And he walked on.

At last Mr. Boo reached the edge of the pond. He couldn't remember how he had known there was a pond here. In any case, here he was. With a groan, he set his fishing rod down on the ground and sat down to rest. I'd never have guessed that fishing is so strenuous. I won't do this again, Mr. Boo promised himself and felt better right away.

He picked up the rod, heaved it up to the level of his shoulder, held it there for a moment, then cast the line. He heard a kind of faint crashing sound. Then he saw that the hook had come to rest a few feet away from him.   What was this? The whole pond was covered by glass. How can I fish when the hook won't even sink into the water? Slowly, he started reeling the line in. But the hook was stuck. He tugged and tugged, pulled and pulled until he got the hook out of the pond.

Now Mr. Boo was as tired as if he had run six miles and then an extra mile. Mr. Boo closed his eyes and hoped that when he opened them again the glass would have disappeared and everything would be just the way it should be when you go fishing. No such luck. When Mr. Boo opened his eyes the pond was still covered by glass. What's more, a strange creature had appeared next to Mr. Boo. It had shiny fur, a wide, flat tail, strong hands and feet, and buck teeth. What is this? Mr. Boo pondered. Then he remembered. A beaver. They have them up in Lapland.

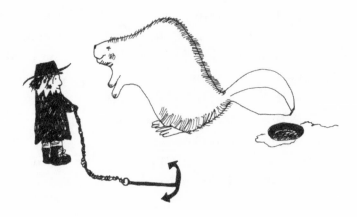

Mr. Boo wasn't able to figure out how the beaver had managed to appear there (and a zoologist couldn't have helped him, either). But he was so tired he didn't care. He scrambled to his feet and took his hat off.

"How do you do?" he said.

The beaver gave him a searching but friendly look. "What are you doing here?" the beaver asked.

"I'm fishing," said Mr. Boo.

"Fishing?"

"Right. But I can't even get the hook to sink into the water, with all that glass on the pond."

"You mean ice," said the beaver, correcting Mr. Boo.

"That's right," said Mr. Boo. When all was said and done he really was a polite person.

"Who are you?" the beaver asked.

"I am Mr. Boo, the wild pitch-black scary really terrifying Mr. Boo," said Mr. Boo but didn't sound too convinced himself.

The beaver was amused but covered its smile with its paws.

"Well, it's day now," Mr. Boo said by way of explanation. Something told him that the beaver was not afraid of him.

The beaver looked at Mr. Boo's fishing rod, at the ice, and again at Mr. Boo. It wanted to ask him something but changed its mind.

"I'll give you a hand," the beaver said.

The beaver used its tail to drill a hole in the ice. It used its tail as if it had been an electric corkscrew, and plop!, before you knew it there was a nice round hole in the ice, with cold black water swirling around in it. Cautiously, Mr. Boo dragged his fishing rod to the edge of the hole and dropped the hook into the water. A whole lot of line disappeared under the ice and then it went slack. Mr. Boo sat down at he edge of the hole. Now I'll just wait for a bite, he thought.

He sat there and waited. He began to feel cold.

"Are they nibbling?" the beaver asked, its face trembling behind its paws in a curious fashion.

"I think they are, but I can't really tell," Mr. Boo replied.

"I'll go down and see," said the beaver and plopped into the hole.

It was gone for a while. Mr. Boo felt colder and colder. He was sure the beaver had somehow got stuck at the bottom of the pond.

"Help!" he shouted. The woods around him answered with a murmur. Mr. Boo felt very small and lonesome. Then the beaver climbed back onto the ice, just as smoothly and quietly as it had dived in. "Go ahead and pull," the beaver said. "It looks like you've got a fish on your hook."

Mr. Boo pulled. He hauled the line in, gritting his teeth, and slowly the hook rose above the edge of the ice. What do you know! From the hook dangled a large, silver-scaled, really quite dead fish.

"Look at that," Mr. Boo said proudly. "Just look at that." The beaver was still shaking as if it had a fever.

"Are you cold? " asked Mr. Boo.

"No, not at all," the beaver managed to say, trying hard not to burst.

Mr. Boo grabbed the fish and tried to get it off the hook but the fish was jammed onto the hook so firmly that he couldn't move it an inch. Mr. Boo shrugged, shouldered his rod and turned around to thank the beaver. But the beaver was nowhere to be seen. Bubbles rose in the ice-hole, and when they reached the surface and burst, they released a little laughter into the air.

Amazed, Mr. Boo stared at the bubbles. Well, the main thing is I got a fish, he thought and started walking back home. He disappeared into the woods with his burden, a fish dangling from a big rusty anchor.

Mr. Boo Receives a Parcel

Mr. Boo woke up because he had a feeling someone was standing in front of his door. Carefully, he put on his coat, tiptoed to the door, and peeked out. Yes, indeed. Right next to the door stood a tall, dark, completely motionless shape. Mr. Boo looked again. The shape hadn't moved. He's lying in wait for me, Mr. Boo thought. Surprise is half the battle! I'll sneak up on him.

Mr. Boo slipped out the window and slowly made his way around the cottage. As he approached the corner of the cottage, Mr. Boo got ready for a tigerish leap, the kind where one gathers all one's strength into one's hind paws. (If one is a tiger.) Mr. Boo tensed the muscles in his legs so hard he almost keeled over. Now!

Roaring like the Siberian tiger in the zoo Mr. Boo pounced on the dark lurking shape. There was a lot of commotion. Mr. Boo lay on the ground. The shape lay beside him, still motionless. Mr. Boo closed his eyes. I won't get up again, he thought. I'm a goner. But nothing happened. Cautiously Mr. Boo opened his eyes. Then he started picking himself up. First he assumed the crawling position of a baby, then he got to his knees, and when the shape still did not pull a knife and attack him, Mr. Boo finally got to his feet. I'm alive, he thought with surprise, and that felt good. I'm sure I'd be much angrier if I were dead.

Then he looked at the shape that rested on the ground, quite unconcerned about his presence. As he pondered what it was he was seeing, the dark shape slowly changed into a long object wrapped in brown paper. It's not alive, Mr. Boo decided. There's something in it. He bent down and started unwrapping it. The strings were tight and Mr. Boo had to fetch a knife from the cottage before he made any progress.

When he'd removed all the paper he saw two long boards with something made out of metal attached to the middle. In addition to the boards there were two sticks that looked like fishing rods with leather straps at one end and small wheels attached to the other end. What on earth are these things? thought Mr. Boo. He was quite nonplussed.

He went inside and in his grandfather's reference library looked for a book that explained strange man-made gadgets. But when he found such a book it was just words, and useless. Besides, it was in German, and Mr. Boo didn't know any German. He put the book back with some effort. It was a heavy book. Then he ran outside again to try to solve the mystery. The boards and sticks lay quietly on the ground.

It was still dark, a typical winter morning. A dim streetlight was still on beside the road. Mr. Boo looked at the pile of paper he had torn off the parcel. There was something white among the brown. Mr. Boo picked it up and raised it to his eyes. TO: MR. BOO, he read with customary ease. These things are for me! But who sent them? Mr. Boo read on. SKIS 1 SET, POLES 1 SET. I've got two too many, there's four objects here. SENDER: ESTF GRDH.

Some foreigner? Mr. Boo thought. I don't know anyone by that name. He wiped the name with his palm to see it better but now all the letters disintegrated and soon there was just a dark blot instead of the name. Now I'll never know who sent me these things and why, Mr. Boo thought, a little sadly.

Mr. Boo looked for his grandfather's old ski boots and put one on. Then he tried to insert the boot into the metal attachment but this turned out to be harder than it looked. Just as Mr. Boo had given up hope he heard a click, and the ski was indeed properly attached to Mr. Boo's boot. He decided to give the other ski to someone as a present. He bent down and picked up a pole. Hey-ho, off we go! The gravel crunched under the ski, the pole punched holes in the dirt, and Mr. Boo kicked wildly with his other foot. Finally, the ski hit an icy spot on the lawn and began to glide. Mr. Boo tried to brake with his other foot, but in vain. Quite soon the ski, the pole, and Mr. Boo lay stretched out on the ground. Mr. Boo's mouth was full of dirt and yellow grass stalks. And he had a pain in his side.

At that point, anyone else would have given up skiing. Not Mr. Boo. Once he decided to do something, he followed through. With some difficulty he got up and once again started scrambling across dead grass and gravel road.

After Mr. Boo had worn himself out, and had fallen down four and a half times (the last time he'd almost managed to stay upright, steadying himself with the pole), he was ready to admit that skiing was not his favorite sport. And even though there were all these stories about how people suddenly grew pale and keeled over at their workplaces because they hadn't exercised enough, Mr. Boo could care less. He was exhausted. Let 'em exercise if they have the strength! I'm so tired I have to get some sleep, thought Mr. Boo.

He bent down to detach the ski from his foot. But the ski refused to come off. Mr. Boo tugged and twisted — to no avail. The ski stayed on. Mr. Boo considered getting a saw, a sledge hammer, a chisel, and an axe, but at that moment a tremendous yawn shook his whole body. I don't think I can deal with this, Mr. Boo thought: I better get some sleep first.

After several attempts to fit the ski through the door he managed to stumble inside. But then the ski wouldn't fit into the bed, no matter how Mr. Boo turned it. He sat down on the edge of the bed, full of heavy sleep, ready to drift off into cloudland. Mr. Boo looked at his foot, at the ski, at the end of the bed. Then he knew what he had to do. He got up and went over to the sofa, picked up two cushions, placed them at the end of the bed and lay down so that the ski remained upright outside the bed. Now it was no longer in the way.

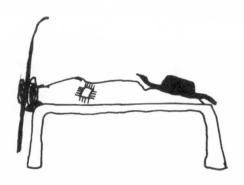

Mr. Boo Scares Rimma

Morning comes, day breaks, night falls. Mr. Boo sleeps and sleeps. In his sleep he meets a dragon wearing Wellington boots, a talking cow that asks him for chewing gum, and his mother who berates him for being afraid of the dark ... and that last one is the nightmare that wakes him up with a start.

The sun shines on the walls and floor of the cottage; it has projected the black window frame onto the floor. Slowly Mr. Boo gets up, walks around the window on the floor, takes care not to step on the glass. It's as if the window had been replaced by a dazzling yellow opening in the wall. The sun shines straight into Mr. Boo's eyes. It takes him a moment to understand that. He is also surprised to find how easy it is to move around. But of course — the ski has fallen off his foot while he was sleeping.

Mr. Boo remembers a dream in which he was skiing across cloud banks and even gliding down a few slopes without falling down. This I'll tell my children, he'd been thinking. If I ever have any.

Mr. Boo walks into the garden and studies the birds. Titmice are flying around his head, one of them alights on his hand. Mr. Boo is amazed that something that moves so fast can weigh so little. The titmouse pecks his hand as if it were a suet ring. Then the birds leave him and fly into the woods. Soon even the sparrows are gone. There is no one on the road. There is no need to hide from anyone. It is daytime, and Mr. Boo stands there, below the tree, all by himself.

"I am the wild Mr. Boo
and the only thing that will do
to tame me is a bright warm day like this.
It makes me melt with bliss,"

Mr. Boo recited to himself. He walked into the shade of the trees. Even though it was the middle of winter it seemed like spring couldn't be far behind: there were big catkins on the willow. Mr. Boo remembered: that means something, it predicts ... but he couldn't remember what. He sat down on a rock but got up quickly when the rock moved and growled "Who disturbs my winter sleep?"

"I didn't know rocks were alive," Mr. Boo said.

"Well, I'm not a rock, I'm a bear camouflaged with moss," said the stone, and sure enough, Mr. Boo saw it turn over onto its other side.

"I'm sorry," said Mr. Boo and walked back to his cottage feeling disgruntled. There was nothing to do. No one to frighten. And he was tired of reading books.

Then he remembered the little cottage in which the little girl lived with her little grand-mother and a cat. Was it possible to frighten children in broad daylight? And what would that feel like? Mr. Boo knew his skills were a little rusty anyway. Perhaps a new attempt would get him going again? Mr. Boo felt pleased. I'll do it, he told himself, then rummaged in his drawers for some useful items. He pulled his hat down over his eyebrows and hit the road.

It was his lucky day: there wasn't a single car on the road, only a bicycle that Mr. Boo didn't even notice before it was right next to him. A large hand appeared at his eye level, holding a round, flat piece of metal with the picture of a lion on one side and the numeral "1" on the other. A rough voice

said: "Go buy yourself something to eat so you'll grow."
Then the bicycle squeaked on, pedaled by a large man.

Without really knowing why, Mr. Boo felt insulted. He put
the round piece of metal in his pocket and decided to add it to
his collection of Trophies from My Expeditions of Terror.
The large man had obviously been afraid of him — why else
give him anything? That thought eased his mind a little.

A thin plume of smoke rose from the cottage chimney. The
spruce trees waved their branches up and down — they didn't
like smoke in public places. But who has ever asked spruce
trees for their opinion on smoking? Mr. Boo snuck up close to
the window and peeked in. Rimma was alone in the room,
playing with her dollhouse. The dolls were having a party.
There were two kinds of cake and buns and little gingersnaps
on their table. The coffeepot was steaming and Rimma was
just pouring coffee into the cup of the doll that looked like the
oldest one: this was the way it was always done.

"Do you take cream and sugar?" Rimma asked.

"I'm on a diet," said the doll, "but if you have some artifi-
cial sweetener, I'll take some of that."

"I'm so sorry, I just ran out," said Rimma.

"Well, it doesn't matter all that much, I can have it without, even though I'm not used to that." And the doll raised her
cup and tasted it.

"Well, this is pretty strong..." the doll said, doubtfully.
"I'll add a little boiled water."

"Rimma's coffee is always real strong," said another doll,
with a knowing nod.

"Can't teach an old dog new tricks," Rimma said, looking
guilty.

Mr. Boo watched all this with a steely stare. He noticed
that he was hungry. Without a sound, he snuck inside. Even

though the window was closed, this was no problem for Mr. Boo. Getting through closed windows was as easy for him as drinking a glass of water.

Mr. Boo pulled a small bundle out of his pocket and set it down on the floor. In a terrible voice he shouted: "WHOOAAAAARRGH!"

Rimma was so scared she dropped the coffeepot onto the new rug. The dolls stiffened in their chairs and stopped talking. They changed into plain old rag dolls stuffed with cotton. Rimma turned around and asked in a faint voice: "Wha-what was that?"

"That was me," Mr. Boo replied proudly and jumped out into the middle of the floor with his hands raised. "Admit that I scared you now!"

When Rimma saw Mr. Boo, her eyes filled with anger, and she grabbed what came to hand, which was a rug-beater, and started beating Mr. Boo with it and shouting:

"You ugly dirty little ghost, get out of here before I really bust you up. You just come here to scare people and to spoil the dolls' coffee party. What a nasty thing to do!"

Now Mr. Boo really was in a tight spot. The only thing he could think of was to use his bundle.

"Look out," Mr. Boo shouted in a loud voice. "See what's jumping around your feet!"

Rimma went rigid — there was a live mouse running around her feet. For some reason Rimma was even more afraid of mice than of Mr. Boo. She had probably learned that from her grandmother.

Now Mr. Boo felt on top of things again, even though his back hurt from the beating Rimma had given him. He drew a deep breath and prepared himself for new attempts to terrify.

But — he had forgotten the cat. Even though the cat hadn't been there the last time (since it had been night and that was when cats roamed), it was here now, and it was a very lively and belligerent cat with an appetite for mice. Without a moment's delay it pounced on the mouse and gobbled it down just as cats have always done in these situations. No lie, it didn't leave a single mouse-hair on the floor. After that the cat licked its whiskers, gave Mr. Boo an incredibly sly look, and went off to curl up somewhere again.

Mr. Boo was struck dumb with rage. One of his most special magical instruments had disappeared forever!

"That cat must be cut open," Mr. Boo said when at last he was able to speak again.

"Cut open!" Rimma shouted and grabbed her rug-beater. "I'll show you cut open! There! And there!"

Mr. Boo whizzed around the room like a black lightning-bolt but Rimma kept up with him. Wherever Mr. Boo managed to run, Rimma was there, ready to swipe him with the rug-beater. Mr. Boo burst into tears of rage and pain. It hadn't been this humiliating the last time.

Then Mr. Boo got too tired to run away and just stood there, resigned, enduring Rimma's swipes like a true philosopher who tells himself at the dentist's: "Pain, you can't touch me!"

Rimma, too, got tired of beating him up. So they just stood there, staring at each other.

Then Rimma picked Mr. Boo up like a kitten, by the scruff of his neck, and carried him to the door. In a mighty arc, Mr. Boo flew into the yard. After he managed to scramble to his feet and slink off toward the shade of the woods, he still heard Rimma's voice behind him:

"Don't you dare bother us again! But if you manage to learn better manners you may come and have coffee with the dolls. We have a party every Wednesday noon. Thank your lucky stars you got off so easy."

Back in his cottage, taking care of his wounds, Mr. Boo went down on his knees and thanked his lucky stars: "Thank you, lucky stars!" And he promised himself he would never again visit that crazy and dangerous little girl. It was a promise Mr. Boo really intended to keep.

Mr. Boo the Magician

It was another day, and Mr. Boo sat at his table and pondered things. During the night, frost had arrived from somewhere, and puddles in the yard glistened like small mirrors. Mr. Boo made tea and hummed a few tunes but didn't manage to cheer himself up much. The walls, squeezed by the frost, made cracking noises. The teakettle steamed on the stove.

Mr. Boo was blue. He thought about his father. Dad had left when Mr. Boo was still a child. All his life Dad had meekly obeyed Grandpa, but one day he got a sudden attack of rage and decided he couldn't spend another moment under the same roof with Grandpa. So Mr. Boo was raised by his grandfather. Nothing had been heard from Dad since, and all Mr. Boo could remember about his mother was a large and welcoming lap and peaceful sleep. Mom had died when Mr. Boo was an infant.

Mr. Boo remembered his Grandpa as a decent man. He had a wide long snowy white beard, dark, somber eyes, and above those, eyebrows as bushy as blackcurrant bushes. Grandpa had led a peaceful life except for now and again when he got excited and transformed the table and chairs into birds or bears or pelicans. One morning Mr. Boo had woken up and noticed he'd spent the night in the lap of a gigantic baboon. That had been Grandpa's way of amusing his grandson. And once, when Mr. Boo had been stubborn the way children often are — nothing odd about that — Grandpa had tossed a stick

on the table and the stick had changed into a snake that began
to wiggle and sing:

"I am a hungry bigmouth snake
   — don't giggle!
I like the taste of little boys,
but even little girls will do:
I eat them both, then sing and wiggle."

Then the snake had made a whistling sound, and when Mr.
Boo got scared his Grandpa had said: "Just grab it." And
when Mr. Boo had cautiously touched the snake, it had
changed into a flute that played little melodies all by itself.
Grandpa had laughed, and that had sounded like someone
kicking a big barrel, hard. Then Grandpa had picked him up,
sung some strange songs with incomprehensible words,
stroked his hair, and taught him first to read and then to do

magic — in matters of magic, it is absolutely necessary to know how to read.

But Grandpa had not taught him how to tell the time. Grandpa had never understood what use clocks were. He said that there was either too much or too little time, depending on how a person felt about it.

Mr. Boo got up, still lost in thought, and took down a thick old leatherbound book with faint lettering on its spine: MOST SECRET AND PECULIAR CONJURATIONS ONLY FOR THE INITIATED. Second Edition. He'd already forgotten some of the instructions but that didn't matter, they were still there in this book.

"How a small bundle can be transformed into a mouse." Mr. Boo blushed with annoyance: that trick was lost forever, buried in the stomach of that awful cat. "How I change night into day." Well, that seemed pretty useless; day and night kept changing into each other anyway. "How I cause a table to change into a bear, a wolf, a fox, a deer." Mr. Boo was heartily tired of those tricks. But what was this, at the top of the next page?

"How I change unhappiness to happiness." Now there are those who say that that isn't magic at all. But it is. Mr. Boo read on: "When you are unhappy, you should go and stand under a tree, close your eyes, count to three and stick your fingers in your ears while saying, Fly away, evil spell, fly away — now begins a new happy day and that should take care of it."

Mr. Boo went outside, stopped by his apple tree and drew deep breaths of the fresh cold air. He closed his eyes, counted one, two, three, stuck his fingers into his ears and said "Fly away, evil spell, fly away — now begins a new happy day" — and at that moment, a little titmouse up on a branch started twittering, and Mr. Boo felt very calm and content. That's how things work when you believe in what you're doing.

Mr. Boo went back in and sat down at the table to read some more. The old book creaked, and the fine dust that rose from its pages made Mr. Boo sneeze. Then he came across this paragraph:

"When it is winter & quite dismal & snow covers the ground, you can change a room into a flowering garden. Would you like tiger lilies, irises, & whale's eyes that hang from trees? This magic formula is extremely secret & has to be read in total silence in the dark."

Mr. Boo closed the curtains so tight that no light entered the room and sat down to go on reading. But now he couldn't see what the book said. Mr. Boo was quite perplexed. Then he thought, well, the book doesn't say anything about total darkness, only total silence. Mr. Boo pulled a box of matches out of his pocket, stopped to listen, and when everything was totally quiet he lit a match and quickly read what the book had to say.

Mr. Boo opened the curtains again and stood there, pondering. This trick could be done if only he could find the right ingredients. This just might work. Mr. Boo went to his grandfather's closet and rummaged in it for a long while. When he appeared again he was covered in cobwebs, dust balls, and wood shavings. In his hand he held a number of small brown bags made out of strong fabric and tied with thick tarry string.

What those bags contained cannot be told, but it may be said that from one of the bags could be heard something like faint cursing, from another, a faint piping sound. One bag rustled as if it contained lizards, another clinked like glass bells in the branches of an elm. Another one weighed so much that

Mr. Boo had to muster all his strength to lift it up onto the table even though the bag was no bigger than a pea-pod.

All day long Mr. Boo boiled, steamed, stirred things, ran about the room like a chicken pursued by a fox, recited spells and sweated. At last, when it began to get dark outside, everything was ready. Mr. Boo found a pale blue candle in the closet, stuck it into a big brass candlestick and lit it with a green Bengal match. Then he waited.

Slowly the candlelight grew brighter and the room emerged from darkness. What appeared first was a big tree, blue and red, from whose branches hung huge eyes that took a close look at Mr. Boo. One of them winked at him. The far wall was covered with yellow irises, and there were tiger lilies everywhere, and they were growling tiger-lilies. The stove had been replaced by a large tree, and the fire glowed from an opening in its trunk. On the branches of this tree there were tiny birds, only about an inch long, and they were skipping around from one branch to the next. In one corner there was a small pond with fish darting about, and on the ceiling shone a huge, wild, golden-yellow moon.

Mr. Boo held his breath, he was so happy. It worked! I did it! Then he began to walk around, cautiously investigating his forest.

He spent the whole night in the forest. And when, as it began to get light outside, the trees and plants and animals slowly changed back into the familiar room, Mr. Boo didn't mind at all, because that was the way it was supposed to be. Now he could, whenever he liked, bring back the magic forest and its creatures — the pike, for instance, that lived in the pond busily baking pastries under a big rock and talking non-stop. That pike had been alone for so long that it simply couldn't stop talking once it got going.

Mr. Boo Loses His
Mirror Image

Mr. Boo was playing solitaire, "Napoleon's Tomb," the way his Grandpa had taught him. But the eight of diamonds never showed up when it should have. Mr. Boo cast a glance to one side and then all around — then, quickly, he rearranged the cards. Now the eight of diamonds came up almost immediately, and soon Napoleon lay in his tomb, surrounded by the four kings. Somehow, Mr. Boo still felt dissatisfied.

"I'm Mr. Boo the Cheater," he said to his mirror image. The mirror image smiled sarcastically but gave no answer.

Then it made a face — but when Mr. Boo tried to grab it, the mirror image disappeared. Mr. Boo found himself staring into an empty mirror.

Now, there really are people who don't have a shadow, and there really are people who don't live inside their bodies; their bodies just walk around hoping to find their selves so they can enjoy life again. If their self has been gone for a long time, only a few manage to find it. So it pays to hold on to one's self.

People without mirror images are rarer, and Mr. Boo had not, in any case, ever heard of such people. He couldn't understand how this could have happened. He closed his eyes and opened them again just a crack, hoping his mirror image would believe that his eyes were still closed and come back to see what was wrong with him. Indeed, something dark and grey could be seen in the mirror: but when Mr. Boo opened his eyes wide again, the mirror was quite empty.

Mr. Boo stood there and pondered. I'll have a cup of tea to perk me up, he decided. I have this funny empty feeling. Mr. Boo rolled up some birch-bark for kindling, stuck it under a couple of logs in the stove, and struck a match. Soon the fire was going well, the water boiled, and Mr. Boo poured it over his Earl Grey tea. After he'd had a cup with a lemon slice and a crumb of sugar, he got up and walked past the mirror as if by accident, then turned his head quickly to catch the mirror image. Some kind of black blot flashed across the mirror — then it was quite empty again. From somewhere far away came the sound of laughter.

Mr. Boo did not panic easily, as a rule, so he didn't panic now. He decided to put the matter out of his mind and to go out to the shed to get some more wood, since there were only a few knotty logs left in the wood-box. Mr. Boo picked those out and left them by the stove, took a basket and opened the door.

Outside, a mild humid southerly wind was blowing. It felt like a foal's muzzle against Mr. Boo's cheek, and there was some new fragrance in the air that made his heart quiver. There were many birds in the trees, singing away fit to burst, and here and there little green spikes stuck out of the steaming black dirt. Along the small open ditch ran a continuous stream of water that carried yellow pine needles, brown leaves, and bits of tree bark. What is this? Mr. Boo asked himself. He knew he had experienced this once before. Well, it'll come back to me. And he walked on to the woodshed.

When he opened the shed door, he had another surprise. In the middle of the floor stood a small cheerful-looking boy with a dirty face. In one hand, the boy held a knife, in the other a piece of bark that looked almost like a boat. He noticed Mr. Boo and gave him a friendly look.

"So this is your place," the boy said.

"Yes, it is," Mr. Boo managed to reply.

"You don't mind, do you, if I carve a bark-boat out of this piece? Nowhere else can you find such great bark," the boy said.

"Are — are you new to these parts?" Mr. Boo asked.

"Yes, we moved here a few weeks ago. From the city. I like it here." And the boy went on carving his boat.

Now, for as long as anyone could remember Mr. Boo's cottage had had such a bad reputation that people avoided it both day and night. Partly, this had to do with the fact that Mr. Boo's Grandpa used to have a little fun at the expense of curious folk who came out to observe him. He turned them into pigs; some he turned into sheep. As you may well image, the women in the region soon put a stop to this: it's no fun to be married to a pig or a sheep.

So, as long as Mr. Boo had been living in the cottage, people had left him alone. Since this was the third shock in a short while, it made Mr. Boo feel faint. He took a few long, deep breaths and sat down on the chopping-block. All of a sudden, Mr. Boo had nothing to say. He just sat there.

The boy looked at Mr. Boo with curiosity.

"My name is Mikko. What's yours?"

"I am Mr. Boo," said Mr. Boo in a slightly unsteady voice.

"Funny name," said the boy. "And, no offence, but your clothes are funny, too. And you're pretty small for a grown-up. But that's all right of course, I mean, as long as you don't mind."

Mr. Boo stared mutely at Mikko.

"I guess you're shy," said Mikko.

> "I am the wild and scary Mr. Boo
> and chicken bones won't do, won't do!
> I boil little children, I fry them, I eat them
> but just for starters,
> I kick them and beat them!"

Mr. Boo declaimed in his scariest voice, getting up and standing tall.

"Now do you recognize me?"

Now it was Mikko's turn to be surprised. It was a little embarrassing when a little old man, none too strong by the looks of him, started spouting such utter nonsense, but since Mr. Boo was red in the face and seemed very serious, Mikko decided it was better to let him believe one was afraid of him. So he said:

"No, please, you scare me when you say such terrifying things."

38

Mr. Boo blushed with pleasure. He strode back and forth a couple of times, then tumbled over a log and fell flat on his face. That tickled Mikko's funny-bone, but he controlled himself and kept a straight face while Mr. Boo brushed stuff off his clothes. Then Mr. Boo climbed up onto the chopping-block, which made him as tall as Mikko, who really wasn't all that short, and said:

"This time I'll let you get away with just that little scare. But don't you dare come again. Because now I'll go and sharpen my knife, and after that, every living thing on this earth better watch out!"

Mr. Boo was shouting now. "I'm telling you!"

Calmly, Mikko finished his bark boat, put a stick in for a mast, a sliver of veneer for the rudder, a piece of bark for a sail. Then he looked critically at his boat.

"D'you think it'll float?" Mikko asked.

Mr. Boo looked at the boat, thought it over.

"A paper sail might work better," he suggested, sounding like an expert.

"You may be right," said Mikko and changed the sail.

They walked outside where the warm sun was shining and buds were swelling in every tree, with the first crocus in bloom on the yellow lawn, and Mr. Boo felt as if decades had suddenly rolled off his shoulders. Mikko walked over to the wide pond and launched his bark-boat. Driven by a light breeze it glided proudly to the other end of the pond, and Mikko picked it up and tried again. Then he looked at Mr. Boo and smiled.

"It's a good one. Thank you," he said.

"By all means," Mr. Boo said.

"I'll be on my way. But — can I come back sometime?"

Mr. Boo gave this some long and stern thought.

"Well, maybe," he said, at last.

Mikko nodded. "Bye, then," he shouted and started running down the road.

"Bye," said Mr. Boo, but Mikko didn't hear him. He had already vanished behind the bend of the road.

Mr. Boo's neck felt warm in the sun. Mr. Boo yawned, filled his basket with logs and carried them inside. Dust motes were dancing in the sunlight, and Mr. Boo considered whether there was any real reason to clean house. Next year is another year, he thought and looked at himself in the mirror.

The mirror image twitched but was no longer able to run away — Mr. Boo had surprised it, by accident, and was now holding it in place with his eyes. The mirror image trembled a little, then adjusted itself to be exactly like Mr. Boo. He opened and closed his eyes a few times to make sure. The mirror image was there and stayed put. Mr. Boo felt sleepy.

"But you're a fraud, nevertheless," he grunted as he stretched out on his bed. A quiet murmur was heard from behind the mirror, but it stopped as soon as Mr. Boo's breathing grew calm and even. And then Mr. Boo rested like a little child, immersed in his dreams.

Mr. Boo Makes a Sacrifice
to the Full Moon

r. Boo woke up in the middle of the night. An irresistible force was pulling him out of bed. Mr. Boo had no choice but to get dressed. He felt anxious. There was a full moon outside, and long narrow clouds were writhing in the sky like black overstuffed snakes. His knife, where was his knife? Mr. Boo re-tied his bootlaces, making the knots tighter. He noticed that he had torn off a scab on his cheek and put a band-aid on the spot. Then, solemnly, he recited the following poem:

> "O great bright greedy moon so full
> By you I swear like a holy martyr
> Mr. Boo won't rest tonight until
> He's found his prey and water."

(Clearly, the water in the last line was meant to represent blood.) Mr. Boo sharpened his knife a little more, then stuck it in its sheath so as not to hurt himself: he had done so once, and nothing much else had happened on that night of the full moon. Maybe, Mr. Boo had thought at the time, it was I who was meant to be the prey. And so he had been able to pursue his calling with a good conscience.

The big moon swam in the sky's blue ink like a round newborn Edam cheese, and the snakes were still swirling around it. The spruce trees sighed, and from one of their branches a great raven flew up to hover in front of Mr. Boo,

41

cawing all the while. Mr. Boo pulled his hat down over his eyes and quietly breezed along the side of the road.

"Prey, prey, run over here,
Here's your little friend so dear!"

There was a rustling sound in the bushes. Now! With a wild roar, Mr. Boo charged the bush, and a little pointy-eared wood mouse just barely managed to slink back into its hole. Mr. Boo growled with disappointment. The wood mouse retired farther into its hole and started cleaning itself. It was famous all over the woods for being a stickler for cleanliness.

Mr. Boo had some trouble getting back on his feet again. His back hurt, he had put it out of whack, somehow. He had also lost his knife: the empty sheath lay on the ground. At last, he found the knife next to a rock: the blade was bent, and the tip had broken off. But on a night of the full moon even a poor knife is better than nothing. Mr. Boo stuck it back in the sheath and continued his journey.

Noises could be heard from beyond the bend of the road. Mr. Boo's instinct told him he was about to find what he was looking for. He gripped the handle of his knife tight and hurried along below the spruce trees without a sound. Now the moon had shaken off the clouds and sailed alone through whistling space.

Down the way Mr. Boo saw two big men. They were punching each other. An old lady lay on the ground, with a basket beside her. By the roadside stood a bottle, which still had some liquid in it. The men looked quite tired but they nevertheless kept pounding on each other as hard as they could, swearing all the time. The mildest cuss-word they used was "dung-face" — it's impossible to even mention the rest. There's two of them, Mr. Boo thought and shrank a little. I'm alone, and my knife is broken and altogether useless. And furthermore, Mr. Boo confessed to himself, I'm scared!

The old lady whimpered a little. The men were fighting over her purse. The old lady had slipped, fallen, and fainted, and the men had happened to pass this way. Since they had been drinking a lot of alcohol, each one of them wanted to keep the loot, and that was why they were pounding each other. Neither one of them had even taken a look at the contents of the purse. It contained two-penny coins, a handkerchief, and a letter from the old lady's sister in Kajaani. And a half-eaten apple. The men had really struck it rich but they didn't know that yet.

The old lady whimpered again. I must save the old lady, Mr. Boo decided. But how? The men were still swearing but sounded tired. Blood dripped off their faces onto the ground. I have to use cunning, Mr. Boo thought. Then he filled his lungs with air, stood stockstill and howled. He howled as loud as he possibly could, and the raven that had followed him accompanied his howl with its cawing.

At once, the men stopped fighting. Looking worried, they listened to the sound.

"That — that'sh a poleesh shiren," one of them said.

"Naw, it'sh jusht some boid," said the other one.

"Oh my Lord — it is the howling banshee!" squealed the old lady whom the yelling had woken up. Then she fainted again.

Mr. Boo mustered all his strength and howled some more, sounding closer and more threatening this time. The raven went Caw Caw Caw.

"Wha' did she shay?" asked the taller of the men and staggered so hard he almost fell down.

"Howling banshee."

"There's no banshees . . ."

Anxiously they stared in the direction of the howl.

"Sheemsh to've gotten closher," the tall one said.

"Maybe we should get outta here," the shorter one whispered.

"I'll take the purshe."

"No, I'll take it."

And they went back to fighting over the old lady's purse. Then Mr. Boo howled a third time from behind a spruce that stood quite close to the road, and that howl was so terrifying he scared himself.

Blindly, the men started running down the road. They left the old lady, the purse, and one of them even left two of his teeth, which he had lost in the fight. They ran and ran until they could run no more and fell down on their faces beside the road, and a patrol car drove by and picked them up for drunkenness. That's how they ended up in jail, after all, if only for one night.

Quietly, Mr. Boo approached the old lady. There was a puddle of blood on the road, and Mr. Boo dipped his broken knife into it and drew some patterns in the air. Then he waved the knife above the old lady and mumbled:

> "Full Moon, here lies your sacrifice!
> Slowly it will decay in the dank dirt.
> Fulfilled are your commandments
> By stone, by stump, by ash and work."

Anxiously the old lady opened her eyes, but when she heard Mr. Boo's magic spell and saw this little man in black waving a knife and sprinkling blood, she fainted for the third time. The old lady was a God-fearing woman who went to church every Sunday morning. She thought she had fallen prey to Satan. How could an old lady like her have known anything about Mr. Boo?

In the top of a spruce, the raven cawed. After he had seen that the old lady was really all right, Mr. Boo went to a pay telephone, dialed three zeroes, and asked for an ambulance. After the ambulance had arrived and howled off again to take the old lady to the hospital, Mr. Boo felt better. Clouds had covered up the moon. Mr. Boo tossed his broken knife into the bushes and walked home slowly.

Mr. Boo Takes a Sauna Bath

One day Mr. Boo got up even earlier than usual. For quite a while he hadn't been sleeping well in the daytime. He had started waking up often, for whatever reason, and in the nighttime he'd been so sleepy he hadn't bothered to work at his job except now and again, and even then more out of habit than desire. Mr. Boo stood and stretched himself, looked around, and was suddenly overwhelmed by the impulse to clean house. He looked at a pile of books over by the back wall. They were a mess, just like his thoughts. Mr. Boo gave them a stern look but they didn't budge. Mr. Boo pondered this, then said:

"One, two, three four five,
Move over there — and look alive!"

The books just lay there, helter-skelter on the floor, quite motionless.

"Shush!" Mr. Boo shouted.

The books were silent. I'm getting old, Mr. Boo thought, sadly. My magic doesn't work anymore. I have to move those books all by myself. And he stuck a book under his arm and lugged it over to the opposite wall. Boy, was it heavy! Mr. Boo started sweating.

He looked at the pile of books. Then he picked up one that looked lighter than the first one — but it, too, was as heavy as a grandfather's sin. Then he picked up the next one, and the next, and the next.

When half the pile had been transferred to the other wall, Mr. Boo sat down on his bed, exhausted. The worst thing was that the new pile of books ... was just as much of a mess as the one on the other side. Instead of one messy pile of books, Mr. Boo now had two of them!

Someone who admires and appreciates the mere number of things might have enjoyed this fact. But Mr. Boo was not of that ilk. What should I do now? He thought and thought. Should I move the rest of the books in the old pile to the new one, or the ones in the new pile back to the old one? He couldn't figure it out.

At last he decided to move the new pile back. And this was how he arrived at that decision:

1. I have already moved them once, so I know how much they weigh.

2. When I carried them over there, the dust fell off them, so they are lighter now. And

3. They looked cozier, somehow, in the old pile.

It was silly of me to decide to move them at all, Mr. Boo thought regretfully. And so he grabbed the nearest book and bravely dragged it back to the old place. And the next, and the next, and the next. When the old pile was the old familiar messy pile of books again, Mr. Boo was so tired that you couldn't find a more tired Mr. Boo in the whole province of Uusimaa even if you added the province of Turku and Pori to it.

Mr. Boo lay on his bed and breathed like one of those foot-pumps for inflating camping mattresses. Besides being tired, he was also covered in dust and dirt from head to toe, filthy like a blanket that's lain on the bottom of a sled in the province of Häme since 1947.

Suddenly Mr. Boo realized that he wanted to get himself clean by whatever means. He pondered what the best way would be.

He could rub sand all over himself. This method, formerly used by Bedouins, wouldn't work because he didn't have enough fine sand here. Snow? There was no more snow. Water? Mr. Boo tried the water in a bucket with his finger, but for some reason it felt cold and unpleasant. Magic? It just wouldn't work again. Sauna?

Sauna? Hmmm.

Mr. Boo picked out a book and read: "This ancient Finnish custom is an excellent restorative for body & soul and has been found especially stimulating when used in conjunction with tar & brandywine."

Why did this sound so familiar? Grandpa had used the sauna — Mr. Boo suddenly remembered that. So there had to be a sauna somewhere in this cottage! Mr. Boo started opening and closing doors. After searching for a while Mr. Boo ended up in a small room in which stood a metal drum filled with black rocks, facing a big wooden bench. All this looked just like the description of a sauna in the book.

Mr. Boo no longer felt tired but newly enthusiastic. I wonder if this sauna still works, he thought with excitement. Following instructions, Mr. Boo pulled out the damper, filled the lower part of the drum with wood, lit it with birch-bark kindling, and closed the oven door. Then he waited.

First he heard the crackling of the wood as it caught fire. Then there was a loud swooshing sound. "It's exploding!" Mr. Boo shouted, covering his face with his hands. But there was no explosion. Instead, the swoosh changed into an even, monotonous hum, and slowly the little room began to heat up. It is working after all, Mr. Boo thought, what a pleasant surprise. Now to get the water. Mr. Boo picked up a bucket and hurried out to the well.

The bucket had little holes in it, so he lost some of the water, but after many trips between sauna and well Mr. Boo had managed to fill a large barrel with as much water as he considered necessary. He put in more wood because the first load had already burnt down to embers, and sweated because it was now quite hot in the sauna. What next? he thought.

The book mentioned a "bath whisk" and said this was made out of birch twigs. Mr. Boo took his broken knife stump (which he had retrieved after a long search) and went into the woods. He climbed on a rock, cut a few birch twigs according to instructions, and tied them into a whisk. It looked just like a broom. Mr. Boo carried his whisk into the sauna, closed the door, and climbed onto the bench.

Now to toss some water onto those rocks! Following the instructions in the book, Mr. Boo took a scoopful of water and tossed it on the rocks on top of the drum.

A tremendous hiss was heard and the water flew back at him — but now it was scalding hot and dirty. Before this happened, Mr. Boo and his clothes had been dirtier than ever before, but now he really looked black — like a doll made out of licorice. (The rocks on the sauna stove were so old that they had turned into fine stone dust and soot. But Mr. Boo didn't know that.)

"Help, I'm frying!" Mr. Boo shouted, but of course no one heard him. Water was running off him like a waterfall. Cautiously, Mr. Boo took off his overcoat and undid his shoelaces. This was worse than summer! Then he took his bath whisk and started using it according to instructions. The book had described how wonderful it felt with the fragrance of birch leaves spreading everywhere and the whisk making the sweat fly off your skin. Vigorously, Mr. Boo applied the whisk to himself, but the only sensation he felt was one of mild pain: his whisk was made out of bare winter twigs and was rather like the "birch" stupid mothers had used in the old days to chastise their children. Fortunately, Mr. Boo was still wearing his shirt and trousers. Had that not been the case he might have hurt himself.

Mr. Boo felt hotter than he'd ever believed possible. He sat on the bench with his mouth open like a fish and panted as if he were about to burst. He'd tossed the whisk somewhere, it hadn't lived up to expectations. What am I supposed to do now? he pondered. Ah, yes: wash and rinse. There was a cake of soap on the bench. Who knows where it came from, but there it was, covered in a pattern of little toothmarks, presumably those of the cottage mouse. Mr. Boo took a small

50

bite and spat it out. Obviously, this soap thing was as useless as the whisk, and Mr. Boo tossed it, too. So. Rinse.

Mr. Boo grabbed the rim of the large barrel and managed to tilt it so the water rushed down on him and his clothes. Mr. Boo squealed like a stuck pig. That water was still pretty much as cold as it had been in the well, and even though Mr. Boo still had some clothes on, it did soak him to the skin. Mr. Boo rushed out of the cottage and stopped in the yard. The world was rocking and swaying in his eyes, and he noticed that he was surrounded by a cloud of steam.

"Help! I'm on fire!" Mr. Boo shouted. True to form, the woods echoed his words. After a while the steam lifted and Mr. Boo saw that he was standing barefoot on the frozen lawn. Strange, he thought, my feet don't feel cold at all. This must be powerful magic.

After Mr. Boo had gone back in, he waited until he and his clothes were quite dry again. Then he went to bed. The bed felt softer than usual and he fell asleep before you could say kiddycat. Mr. Boo slept for two days and two nights and dreamed things he forgot immediately. That's the way it tends to be — good dreams don't last into the daylight, they like the dark too much.

Mr. Boo and the
Building Contractors

On his way to the shed, Mr. Boo heard a loud noise in the nearby woods. That was an explosion, Mr. Boo thought and froze as if he had swallowed a fence post. The noise was followed by a loud din, the sound of an engine, the sound of breaking branches. What was going on? Mr. Boo set his basket down on the floor of the shed and stepped outside.

In a small grove of trees he saw three men and a caterpillar. The men had just started drilling a hole straight down into the ground. Next to them there were other holes opened up by the explosion. When they were done drilling, the men pulled the long drill-bit out of the ground, drew a number on it, and placed it on the trailer. Then they repeated the whole thing thirty feet farther away. The drill-bits piled up on the trailer. Then the men took a break. They unbuttoned their workshirts and smoked cigarettes (they must not have known that tobacco is a killer poison, or else they had started smoking when they were very young and had become so used to tobacco that they were beyond redemption . . .) and had a quiet conversation.

"This looks like a good site," said the first man.

"The one back there didn't seem too bad, either," said the second.

"It was better," said the third.

"But this is solid ground, here," said the first.

"It's not waterlogged," said the second.

"No, that it ain't," said the third.

"Good site for a house," said the first.

"Sure enough," said the second.

"No problem," said the third and blew his nose. "But it won't be easy to build the road here, across that swamp and the pond."

Now Mr. Boo became horrified. Listening to the men's talk, he realized that they were checking the ground in order to see if they could build a house on it.

If it hasn't already been understood, it must be understood now that the likes of Mr. Boo don't feel comfortable in regions where houses start popping up like mushrooms and less and less space is left for woods and meadows. When this happens, they have to look for new places to live, and when you consider that they are short on ready cash and don't know any real estate agents, it becomes clear that they have an even harder time finding a new place to live than do ordinary people for whom that is no picnic, either. The numbers of Mr. Boos dwindle wherever dwellings multiply, especially when these are constructed in the form of tall foursquare boxes in which people have to huddle the rest of their lives as if they were already buried in an Italian cemetery.

Listening to the men, Mr. Boo understood that these were the kind of buildings they had in mind.

"Well, let's go," said the first man when he had finished smoking his poison.

"All right," the second and third one said in unison, and the caterpillar started growling and shaking across the moor, crushing many small pine saplings into the ground with its treads. There are no laws against that kind of killing; no one has managed to translate the language of pines into human language, and people really don't seem interested in such translations anymore.

Mr. Boo sat on a tree stump and pondered. Here and there, the ground was bare, even though it was only late January. Nature is as unpredictable as the future, Mr. Boo thought. I have to move. But that's impossible — I can't even put my books in order! So, I have to stay. But how can I stay if they put up a building here?

What should I do?

Mr. Boo sat and pondered. Sat and pondered. It was getting dark, and the short winter light disappeared as if covered up by one layer of gauze after another. Mr. Boo felt cold, but the question was too important for him to give up. He remembered what the men had said. "This is solid ground," one had said. "Not water-logged," said the other. Water-logged. If the ground were water-logged, would that help me? Yes, it would, because the men had also complained about the pond and the swamp. Would it be possible to channel some of the pond water here? The pond wasn't all that close by, and Mr. Boo was a small person. The mere thought of trying to dig a ditch from the pond to these sample drill holes in the ground seemed absurd. It would take him a year. Grandpa's magic wouldn't work here, either. I need some help, Mr. Boo thought in despair. But who? Who do I know ...

"You know me," said a voice next to his ear. The beaver stood on its strong hind legs and looked at Mr. Boo with a friendly expression.

"Oh yes," said Mr. Boo and tried to remember when he had met the beaver.

"That time you went fishing," the beaver said helpfully.

"That's right, of course," said the omniscient Mr. Boo and felt even more surprised because he couldn't remember ever having gone fishing.

"I'll help you," said the beaver and vanished again.

Mr. Boo called his name but he was nowhere to be seen. Strange. Now it was really dark but Mr. Boo's night vision was as good as a bat's, perhaps even better. Then, just as suddenly as he had disappeared, the beaver appeared again.

"Come along," the beaver said and trotted off. Mr. Boo followed. He had nothing to lose.

When they came to the edge of the pond, which had melted in the unseasonally warm weather, the beaver began to cut down tall pines to dam up the brook that ran from the pond. The speed with which he did this was incredible. The beaver put his teeth up against the pine trunk, switched himself on like a chainsaw, and bzzzz, the tree was down.

After a while the brook was dammed up and the water spread out in the woods. And where did it run? Precisely in the direction of the planned building site!

Mr. Boo watched. He was at a loss for words. The beaver sat down to wait. The water filled the holes in the ground and spread over a large tract of the woods. Then it started freezing, in some places so quickly that one could see it happening. When there was enough water in the woods, the beaver dismantled the dam, and the water from the pond flowed in the brook just as before.

"That's so they won't notice where the water came from," the beaver explained. Then he grinned. "I'm in no hurry to acquire new neighbors, either," he said and disappeared. Mr. Boo didn't even have a chance to wish him a good morning.

The night passed. In the morning, the sound of an engine was heard again. Mr. Boo hid behind a rock and waited. Out of the woods came the noisy caterpillar and with it the three men plus a small ruddy spherical man who bossed the others around. They called him Mr. Engineer but pointed at him and made faces behind his back. The caterpillar stopped and the men jumped down.

"This is the site?" the engineer asked.

"This is it," said the men.

"Are you out of your minds?" asked the engineer in his softest voice. "This place is under water."

The men looked around and were amazed. During the night, the ice had melted, and there was water glittering everywhere between the tussocks.

"This can't be," said the first man.

"This can't be the same place," the second one said.

"It can't," said the third.

"And yet it is the same place," the first one said.

"So it is," said the second.

"It can't be helped," said the third. "But there was no water here yesterday."

The engineer turned turkey-purple and started yelling.

"You must have been (expletive) drunk as (expletive) skunks. (Expletive.) I won't (expletive) let you (expletive) get away with this."

He went on for a good while. The men looked dazed. Then they shrugged and turned the caterpillar around and slowly drove back through the woods the way they had come. They ignored the engineer. His yells could be heard for quite some distance. Then the woods were quiet again.

Mr. Boo made his way home. Strange, how friendly the pines looked today, and how soft the moss felt underfoot. Birds fluttered past Mr. Boo's head, and in the birch grove a flock of magpies sounded like a threshing machine. The wind carried a whiff of burning wood through the air. Somewhere a dog barked. Mr. Boo had no complaints.

Mr. Boo Goes to Town

It was night, and Mr. Boo was wandering back and forth in the woods. The mice were asleep, the birds were asleep, the bats were hibernating, even the trees were asleep. But Mr. Boo couldn't bring himself to go home. He felt restless and driven for no reason he could understand. There are times when you just have to follow your nose.

An old van stood by the roadside. Something was being unloaded from it and taken to a small house. A bit of yellow light shone through the blinds of two windows that looked like the eyes of a half-asleep cat. Before he knew it, Mr. Boo had climbed into the empty rear of the van and hidden himself between two barrels. At the same moment someone sat down in the driver's seat, turned on the ignition, switched on the lights, turned on the windshield wipers, shifted into first and gave gas. The van was on its way, and Mr. Boo was going with it.

There were times when Mr. Boo was scared, but this wasn't one of them. To tell the truth, Mr. Boo enjoyed the sensation of speed. He had never been in a motor vehicle before. Hey, he thought, step on it! With delight he watched, from the back window, the road slip away like a conveyor belt. I don't believe this, he said to himself.

After a while the van stopped, the way all motor vehicles in this world do, either because they have run out of gas, or because there's something wrong with the engine, or because a destination has been reached. Mr. Boo came to a halt as well. Calmly he waited for further developments. Since the van didn't start up again, Mr. Boo decided to get out. He opened the door and did just that.

The van had taken him to the city. Mr. Boo had never been there before but had heard and seen the buildings of the city spread like witches' broom in a diseased birch grove. Now he just stood there and stared, his eyes like brass rings. It was quiet because it was two o'clock in the morning of a working day. All around him, dark stonewalls rose up to the sky, their windows dark with few exceptions — so few that they just made the buildings look even lonelier.

Mr. Boo could hear a distant car and the muffled footsteps of some lonely wanderer. The streets were covered in brown mud, sand, and oil stains. The trees looked nauseous, and here and there stood some dead pines. In dark corners unseen by human eyes Mr. Boo saw hordes of rats who were busy building their thousand-year empire the way their ancestors had done before them. Mr. Boo felt faint. Even though his mental image of the city had been on the dark side, he hadn't expected anything so appalling.

(On the other hand, we don't all share Mr. Boo's tastes. If you look for warmth and comfort, pleasure and people, these can be found in the city. But there was no way Mr. Boo could have known that.)

Mr. Boo walked the empty streets and looked around. Shops, signs, leafless shrubs, parks to walk dogs in, chicken coops, dairies, statues, hamburger joints, bacon, soup, chocolate milk, strawberries, poor people's food, wealth, misery, money, too many delicacies, rotten fish, offal, dirt, piles of stuff, shells of people; all this he saw, Mr. Boo, and no one else but him saw it just then.

How will I ever get home again? Mr. Boo thought, on the verge of tears. I don't even know where I live! He tried to remember his address but all he came up with were words his Grandpa had used: in the Pine Woods ... past the Devil's Pond ... That wasn't enough to ask for directions. Why did I get into that van, thought depressed little Mr. Boo.

When the need is great, help is not always at hand. Mr. Boo ran up one street and down another, to the harbor and the empty marketplace, hurried past the President's Palace and the Guard House and the small ships by the landings, suddenly found himself in the perennial din of the railroad station, and finally hid in a small park to catch his breath. All along he hadn't seen a single person. There had been a light on in one of the windows of the President's Palace. Maybe the President had taken off his false bald pate and sat there secretly brushing his long dark luxurious hair? And yes, here and there he had seen policemen standing on streetcorners, looking like rubber dolls. In the basin by the marketplace there had been a few ducks.

But what about these automobiles with a yellow light on top with the word TAXI on it? There were a lot of those cruising around. Would they be of any use? Mr. Boo thought the policemen looked too forbidding, so he decided to hail a TAXI. As soon as he'd timidly raised his hand, one of them came to a screeching halt beside him. Its door flew open. Mr. Boo climbed in and the cab took off immediately. The driver cast an absent-minded glance at Mr. Boo. That evening and night he had, once again, seen all the kinds it takes to make a world. Nevertheless, Mr. Boo was a new addition to his people collection. But the driver wouldn't have been particularly surprised if his new passenger had been a sixteen-foot male with pink hair down to his ankles and the tusks of an elephant. He had seen a bit of the world.

"Where to?" he asked, casually.

"The Pine Woods ... past the Devil's Pond," whispered Mr. Boo. He was so scared that this was the best he could do.

"OK." And the cab made a screeching U-turn and headed out of town.

Mr. Boo understood nothing. Did this man know where he lived? Or were there many places in the world with the same name? Well, he'd find out. And why was this man giving him a ride, anyway?

After a while, this vehicle, too, came to a stop. The driver switched off the gizmo that had been ticking on the dashboard, looked at it and said: "Thirty-two marks."

"I see," Mr. Boo said politely.

"Thirty-two marks. Money."

"Money?" said Mr. Boo.

"Dough, moola, pesetas, shekels, coin," the driver said helpfully while suspecting he'd come across a deadbeat once again. What's more, this filthy little creep seemed to be an imbecile.

"Where — where does one usually find money?" Mr. Boo asked in a frightened tone.

"Just check your pockets, buddy. Or we'll go for a ride to the precinct."

Mr. Boo wanted to ask the man what a "precinct" was but didn't dare and started going through his pockets. After a while he had collected many scraps of paper, an old book, and a leather coin purse. He handed all of it to the driver. The driver looked at it for a moment, tossed the paper scraps out the window (and thus destroyed, unbeknownst to himself or Mr. Boo, the only surviving Formula for Achieving Invisibility Without Much Effort), and turned the pages of the book which he realized was a rare first edition from the eighteenth century. The driver was a member of a bibliophiles' association. Then he opened the coin purse and shook the contents into his palm.

Out rolled five dark yellow coins the size of a full moon on the horizon. The driver let out a long whistle, turned the coins in his fingers, then looked at Mr. Boo.

"Gold?" he asked.

"Ye-es?" Mr. Boo said, shakily, still completely nonplussed.

The driver's eyes lit up. He palmed one of the coins. Reluctantly, he put the remaining four into the purse and handed the purse and the book to Mr. Boo who shoved them in his pockets trying to prepare himself to endure things to come. But the driver just opened the door for Mr. Boo and said:

"Thank you, sir. Hope to see you again soon. It's been a pleasure."

Mr. Boo nodded. Utterly confused, he headed toward the woods where he found first one trail and then another and finally a third, and after he had followed it for a while he saw his cottage waiting for him. It wore a chilly expression because it hadn't been heated for many hours.

Mr. Boo hurried to light a fire and make some hot tea. He was so confused by everything that he wasn't able to think about anything in particular. It had surprised him a little that the driver had been so delighted with the contents of the coin purse. Grandpa's chests down in the cellar were full of those things. At some point, Grandpa had collected a lot of them from God knows where, but Mr. Boo had never cared for them — he'd much preferred pine cones to play with. But now a use had been found for them. If the cab driver liked them, other people probably did, too. Who knows what they're really good for, thought Mr. Boo, but forgot that thought immediately. He really couldn't care less.

The water came to a boil on the stove, and Mr. Boo made tea and let it steep. He went to a cupboard and helped himself to some zwieback from a seemingly inexhaustible supply. He stirred a pinch of sugar into his tea and nibbled on the zwieback. The winds of winter swooshed around the corners of the cottage. The light of the fire in the stove radiated out into the room and flickered on the floor and the walls. For a long time Mr. Boo sat there, staring into the flames.

Mr. Boo and the Enormous Cat

Mr. Boo strode back and forth in his cottage and sang:

"Poor and friendless, all alone
I dwell here in this world
And even though I know this is so
That doesn't console me at all."

In this manner, an hour passed, and then another. Slowly Mr. Boo calmed down. It was a night in early spring, and it was snowing outside so things would look white in the morning. Mr. Boo was in a good mood. He looked at the lingonberry shrub he had dug up and put in a vase. It had a little greenish fuzz and white buds the size of the head of a pin.

"When you're ready, I'll pick your berries and eat them," Mr. Boo told the little blossoms and enjoyed the foretaste of lingonberry jam.

Mr. Boo would have to wait a long time for that to happen. Well, he had time. The tea water bubbled on the stove. Mr. Boo had some tea and considered going to bed. No point in going out to scare children in a raging blizzard. They'd soon be waking up anyway.

There was a crash on the roof, followed by a thump. The wind, Mr. Boo said to himself.

Then there were heavy footsteps. The wind is walking, thought Mr. Boo and helped himself to another cup of tea.

Then it sounded like something heavy had fallen off the roof. Whatever it was, it made a shrill yowling sound. Then something pounded on the door.

Now Mr. Boo was a little surprised. A walking wind that falls off the roof and pounds on the door? he thought. Well, live and learn.

Mr. Boo took a book from his shelf and started studying it. Only after a little while he noticed he was holding it upside down. He had thought it was written in Arabic.

Then there was more pounding on the door, and a hoarse voice shouted:

"Let me in or I'll break the door down!"

Mr. Boo got up to open the door. He picked up a poker and held it behind his back, determined to teach this wind some manners. If it was a southerly, easterly, or westerly wind, he'd show it what was what. But if it was a wind from the north, he'd have to be a little more careful, because that was a cold one, and if it got angry it might keep on blowing around his house for years on end. Then again, how will I know what sort of wind it is? I've never seen one, Mr. Boo thought and opened the door a crack.

The door flew open and Mr. Boo retreated to the other end of the room: in the doorway stood an enormous black cat. It miaowed and asked him in an unpleasant voice:

"Are you alone?"

"Yes, I am," Mr. Boo said. "Mom and Dad aren't home yet." He didn't know why he had said that, but it had seemed appropriate.

"Good," said the huge cat and stepped inside, running the tip of its tail across the ceiling. It stopped in the middle of the room, looked around with a mean expression, and asked:

"Aren't there any little children here — I mean, except for you?"

"No, there aren't," said Mr. Boo, clutching his poker.

"No mice?" asked the cat.

"No mice," Mr. Boo said firmly.

"Not even a little drop of milk?" the cat asked in an even angrier tone.

"No," said Mr. Boo. His voice trembled. "There's just a little tea, and I just finished it."

And he finished his cup with lightning speed.

"Sssss," the furious cat hissed. "Then I'll eat you."

"But why?" asked Mr. Boo, looking very surprised.

The cat looked surprised, too. It thought things over for a minute.

"Because I'm used to eating small children," it then said, licking its chops. "They taste so good."

Here we have to remind ourselves that Mr. Boo himself was big on scaring children: but even though he threatened to turn children into steaks, he had never even imagined that it was really possible to eat them. That was just a figure of speech. Everybody knew that.

"You are mad," Mr. Boo said, sternly. The enormous cat's eyes narrowed to slits.

"No one calls me that. I didn't hear that," it said and arched its back.

Then the cat opened its mouth and showed its teeth. They looked like knives. Very slowly, the enormous cat advanced on Mr. Boo. Mr. Boo racked his brains. The cat approached so smoothly that it didn't seem to be moving — but its jaws came closer and closer. It took another stride.

"Why are you so big?" shouted Mr. Boo. He couldn't think of anything else to ask.

"Why are you so small?" the cat asked in a saccharine voice. "And besides, I'm not too big. It's you who is too small. And soon you'll be even smaller!"

The cat opened its mouth to devour Mr. Boo.

Mr. Boo sprang into action. He flung the poker into the cat's maw and dived under his bed where he closed his eyes and ears and expected the worst.

He couldn't hear anything, but then remembered he had stuck his fingers in his ears. When he took them out, he heard a noise that sounded as if his cottage had been the target of aerial bombardment. He peeked out and saw the huge cat bouncing all over the floor. The poker had stuck sideways in its mouth, and it was unable to get it out. It was clawing tracks into the floor as deep as ski tracks in fresh snow. It wasn't any less threatening than it had been before. I have to think of something else, thought Mr. Boo, trembling under the bed.

Suddenly he remembered his childhood and how he'd sat on Grandpa's lap and how Grandpa had taught him to do magic. Grandpa had sung in a deep voice and changed things into animals. Mr. Boo still knew how to do that. But how to change animals into things? Grandpa had taught him that, too, but Mr. Boo couldn't remember, and there wasn't a whole lot of time left because the cat was already tearing up his bedding as if it were kleenex.

Then Mr. Boo remembered. First you recited the spell and then you repeated it backwards. And Mr. Boo spoke the spell and reversed it: "Down, terrible cat! Tac elbirret, nwod! Turn into white milk! Klim etihw otni nrut! One two three! Eerht owt eno!"

Nothing happened at first. Mr. Boo thought he was done for.

But then a hiss was heard, and slowly the huge cat melted away and became just a little puddle of milk on Mr. Boo's rug.

Mr. Boo found it hard to believe that such an old spell could have been so effective. Cautiously he crawled out from under the bed and walked over to the puddle of milk. The puddle didn't budge. The enormous cat was nowhere to be seen.

Mr. Boo got a rag and wiped up the puddle. He thought for a moment, then tossed the rag into the stove. There was another hiss, a distant miaow, and the smell of burnt milk. Then something went whoosh in the stove and a draft of air threw Mr. Boo toward the door and made the ceiling lamp swing. After that, all was quiet.

When Mr. Boo looked out it was morning and on the new clean snow there were paw prints the size of big fists. They led over to the rose hedge and disappeared down the road.

The first sounds of traffic could be heard in the distance. I was saved from terrible danger, Mr. Boo thought and felt really scared for the first time that night. It could have eaten me. How can a cat get so big? I don't understand.

Then he saw that there was another set of cat tracks in the snow, but these were small: they ended under Mr. Boo's window where they suddenly became huge and proceeded up the ladder. Mr. Boo walked over and bent down to take a closer look. He brushed some snow off a torn pouch with a little bit of green powder on the bottom. The cat had been eating it.

Now Mr. Boo understood. While cleaning out his closets he had thrown out some of Grandpa's old pouches, thinking they were too old to have any magic left in them. But this one had worked, all right. What if I tried it myself? I'd grow as tall as the tallest tree, Mr. Boo thought.

He raised the pouch to shake the remaining powder into his mouth but changed his mind in the nick of time.

He pocketed the pouch and sat down to think things over. That was a close shave. If I had become big, where would I have gone to live? Where would I have found food? Everybody would have seen me, I wouldn't have been able to hide anywhere. Imagine! I almost made a terrible mistake. Mr. Boo felt faint just thinking about it.

Back inside, Mr. Boo hurried to toss the pouch into the stove. It flared up for a moment, burned with a sputtering green flame. Then it was gone. Mr. Boo congratulated himself as if he'd just been saved from death by drowning.

Mr. Boo Goes to a Party

Mr. Boo got scared because some huge black thing came sliding toward him and was about to suck him up. Mr. Boo struggled with all his might, but to no avail, the black creature had already swallowed his body — only his head remained outside.

"Help," Mr. Boo shouted, "help me!"

But no one came to the rescue. The world was white and empty. Now his head, too, started slipping inside the thing. Mr. Boo mustered all his strength to get free, and hey presto, he woke up in his own bed.

Bright sunshine poured in through the curtains, and he could hear the titmice twitter. Spring is coming on, Mr. Boo thought. He couldn't remember how he knew that. There was still a lot of snow outside. Only a little while ago the ground had been bare, and the trees had been budding. It had looked like winter wouldn't come at all. Now it had come, but spring was also on its way.

Once Grandpa had told him about a year when you could drive sleds across frozen lakes in June, but Mr. Boo had dismissed this as one of Grandpa's tall tales. In June one could go swimming along the muddy shore. Not me, though, Mr. Boo reminded himself. He was no swimmer. In fact, his water skills were those of a stone.

He closed his eyes, but then it occurred to him that if he fell asleep again, that big black thing would return and devour him ... It had been a memory of the enormous cat. Even though Mr. Boo was quite certain that the enormous cat had burned up in the stove, it was also true that huge paw-prints had appeared in the snow after that event. I mustn't go on thinking about that. If I don't think about it, it doesn't exist. There is no enormous cat. It doesn't exist. But if it should come while I'm asleep ... Now I thought about it again. I have to think of something else. But what?

The sun was shining. It was great ski weather. No, I won't ski ever again. Or I could build a snow fort, but that's really strenuous ... I could read something, but all these books are so familiar. I could go visit friends.

Friends? I don't have any friends, thought Mr. Boo. Then he remembered what little Rimma of the little cottage had said:

"If you behave yourself you can come and have a cup of coffee."

What if I went there? Mr. Boo thought and pulled on his jacket. I could bring her a surprise. He started thinking about what that could be. After searching his drawers for a while he found what he'd been looking for. He wrapped it in a hand-kerchief and stuck it in his pocket. He was ready to go.

Outside it was altogether too bright. The snow glittered as if a thousand bottles had been smashed into tiny splinters that had then caught on fire. Terrified, Mr. Boo closed his eyes but kept walking. Bang! He was flat on his back on the ground. A big bump swelled up on his forehead. The apple tree with which he'd collided was angry, too. It didn't feel too good anyway. What a spring, the apple tree thought.

"Sorry, my fault," Mr. Boo mumbled and headed toward the shade of the woods, rubbing his eyes. One of his boots sank into a snowdrift, and his feet began to feel cold. I should have stayed in bed and told my fortune with my cards, thought Mr. Boo. But he had already walked so far that it was pointless to turn back.

Rimma's cottage huddled in the snow, busy keeping warm. Its eyes were frosted over, and a strong straight pillar of smoke rose from the chimney. The yard had been swept. There were small animal tracks in the snow. A big crow swept down from the top of a spruce, flew right over Mr. Boo and swung away again: he was a little too large to be considered prey.

Mr. Boo shivered. Cautiously he knocked on the cottage door. When no one answered, he knocked again. Finally he opened the door and stepped inside. I need to warm up in any case, he thought, or else I'll turn into a snowman and won't thaw out until spring.

There was a hubbub of voices in the other room. So she is here. I better not make any noise so I won't scare Rimma, Mr. Boo thought. Then he felt ashamed. I've become far too kind to children. I'll be out of a job if I go on like this.

He straightened his back and yanked open the door to the other room. As soon as the children saw Mr. Boo, they started screaming their heads off. They scattered quickly, dashed away, hid themselves here and there. When the screaming stopped, Mr. Boo realized that frightened children's eyes were watching him from under the sofa and the table, from the closet, from behind the curtains. Now the room was silent as a tomb. You could hear thoughts conversing with each other.

Mr. Boo's chest swelled with pride. They are afraid of me, he thought. I haven't been this effective for many years. He grew at least ten inches taller, he was so full of himself.

Then he heard an angry intake of breath, and Rimma said in a hard voice:

"It's you again. I told you not to come and scare me again! Now you'll get a spanking you'll remember the rest of your life." And she came toward him with a threatening expression. Quickly Mr. Boo shrank to his normal size.

"I didn't mean to scare you," he said timidly.

"You didn't? Are you sure?" Rimma looked at Mr. Boo to see if he meant what he said.

Mr. Boo blushed. He had to admit it. Never! But he had to. And he said, so quietly that the others couldn't hear him:

"I really didn't. I even brought you a present."

He took out his handkerchief bundle and gave it to Rimma. Rimma took the bundle and examined it closely. One after the other, the children came out of hiding. Mr. Boo recognized one of them: it was the boy who had carved a boat in his woodshed. Mikko, too, remembered Mr. Boo and immediately forgot his fright.

"Oh, it's you, is it? You're nothing to be afraid of. I thought you were some horrible bogeyman. Hello!" And he held out his hand to Mr. Boo.

Mr. Boo blushed again. He was so furious he felt like bursting. But he just had to grin and bear it. Mr. Boo started sweating. Since Mikko was still holding out his hand, Mr. Boo had to do something. Without thinking, he took Mikko's hand, and Mikko held his hand in his own for a moment and then let go of it. So, what's next, Mr. Boo thought. But he felt relieved: Mikko's gesture hadn't meant the beginning of a fight.

Rimma was untying the handkerchief. The other children gathered around. Soon they would see what was in the bundle. But no ... It was just a little old piece of wood.

The children sighed, disappointed. Rimma swallowed her annoyance and held out her hand to Mr. Boo. It was proper to thank a person for a present, and that little black fellow

74

looked as if he'd given her something valuable even though it was only a piece of wood. Perhaps it had some value to him. Mr. Boo gave her his hand, and Rimma squeezed it. Just to see what would happen, Mr. Boo squeezed hers back.

"Ouch," Rimma cried, in pain.

"Sorry," Mr. Boo mumbled, gripped by panic.

Rimma dropped the piece of wood on the floor and sobbed. At once, the piece of wood started growing and changing its shape. The children rushed to the walls of the room. What on earth was it going to be?

A big black and white bird rose up from the floor. It glided around the room with soft soundless wingbeats, then settled on Rimma's shoulder and began to sing.

Rimma forgot her sobs and listened, enchanted. Mr. Boo was just as surprised: this piece of wood was supposed to turn into a baby doll. But it was true that Grandpa had never labeled things right. From now on, I better test everything first, so I'll know what becomes what. It's a good thing this didn't turn into a snake. This girl would have killed me. Mr. Boo drew a breath of relief.

75

"What's its name?" Rimma asked him.

"Birdie," said Mr. Boo. He couldn't think of another name.

"Birdie, birdie, birdie," the children repeated. The bird sang and the children started humming along. Soon the whole room was filled with soft singing and sunshine. Mr. Boo felt right at home. This was really nice. At least, it was nicer than skiing. Or fishing, for that matter. Even fishing didn't quite match this.

"Will it always be a bird?" Rimma asked suddenly.

"Always when you want it to," Mr. Boo said. He flicked the bird's beak with his middle finger and it was instantly transformed into a piece of wood. Then he flicked the other end of the piece of wood, dropped it on the floor, and once again a big bird rose into the air and flew up to Rimma's shoulder. Rimma flicked its beak and then it was a piece of wood again. She put it in her pocket.

"Great," Rimma said. "What's your name?"

"I am Mr. Boo," Mr. Boo said and blushed for the third time. He believed that all the children in the neighborhood knew his name.

"I am Rimma."

"I remember," said Mr. Boo, a little embarrassed. Rimma paid no attention to him but took out her piece of wood again, flicked it, dropped it on the floor, and once more the room was filled with black and white wingbeats and deep, flute-like song.

"Would you like something to drink?" Rimma asked Mr. Boo. "I've got this really great blueberry juice."

Mr. Boo admitted that he was thirsty.

"And here's a little bit of cake, too," Rimma said and stuck a chunk of some strange sticky stuff in Mr. Boo's mouth. "I baked it myself."

Mr. Boo's eyes bulged. This pasty stuff tasted terrible. He tried to swallow it, then tried to chase it down with a glass of juice and had a tremendous coughing fit because the juice had gone down the wrong pipe. Mr. Boo seriously thought he was going to die. This was worse than the enormous cat. I can't understand why I was so afraid of it, Mr. Boo thought and coughed and coughed.

When he finally managed to open his eyes and breathe again, the children started playing cops and robbers. Mr. Boo was a cop, of course. The children pelted him with pine cones, eggs, and juice. Then they played blind man's buff. Mr. Boo was blindfolded and tripped or else had cold water poured down his back. After that came "shopping," and Mr. Boo was relieved of all his gold coins, but these didn't impress the children any more than they impressed him. (Rimma's grandmother, however, practically fainted when she saw them the next day.) Finally, Mr. Boo was beaten up with pillows and kicked in the legs. This was known as a "pillow fight." Mr. Boo had never had such a going-over in his life. At the end, Mikko punched Mr. Boo in the ribs and said: "That's just to show that we're all buddies now. So you'll remember."

Mr. Boo wasn't able to say a word because his mouth was still full of Rimma's cake, which he couldn't get down but couldn't spit out either for reasons of politeness. He sat on the edge of the bed, tried to breathe through his nose, and panted like a hound. The bird flew around the room and sang. The children had started covering Mr. Boo with little shreds of newspaper and were tying his legs to the table. The noise was worse than at a county dance at midsummer. Mr. Boo tried to act unconcerned. Then Rimma came up to him and gave him a big hug that took his breath away.

"I think you're terrific," Rimma said.

Mr. Boo blushed for the fourth time, turning the color of strawberry jam. The children gathered around him and looked at him with serious expressions.

"What if he dies now?" asked the smallest child. "He's so red in the face."

"Nah, people don't die of that," said Rimma.

Motionless and poker-faced Mr. Boo sat on the edge of the bed and didn't say anything. Then he got up and nodded his thanks and headed for the door.

The string around the table leg tightened. But Mr. Boo didn't notice anything. Looking dignified, he approached the door. The children behind him giggled ...

That evening the moon shone bright above Mr. Boo's cottage. Mr. Boo limped over to the stove and sipped his tea. He remembered how he had taken a tumble. Suddenly he smiled at the mirror and the mirror image smiled back, cautiously, because it had never seen this expression on Mr. Boo's face. Mr. Boo was feeling no pain. He smiled again, shook his head, and moved around the room enjoying his memories of the day's events.

Mr. Boo Meditates on Life

Mr. Boo stirred the fire in the iron stove. He watched the turning embers spread their red glow. The warmth of the burning wood had saturated the stove, and the water kettle was steaming. The night was quiet. From somewhere far off a dog's bark was heard for a while, then it faded away. Mr. Boo didn't feel like going anywhere or doing anything special. He just sat there and cogitated.

Soon another year will be over, Mr. Boo thought. A lot has happened. I really don't feel like going out and frightening children anymore. Why should I work so hard when I can get by with less? No one is going to reprimand me even if I don't do anything. It's nobody's business but mine.

The night outside was bright, the stars twinkled in the sky. Mr. Boo knew that the stars and constellations had all kinds of names like The Bull, The Twins, The Big Dog, The Bearward, The Coachman, The Whale, The Small Bear, The Snake Carrier, The Chisel, The Goldfish, The Furnace. One of those stars was a hundred thousand times the size of the sun. Another, whose light could still be seen, had in fact exploded and gone dark. It was just that it was so far away that the light still kept coming. At some time when Mr. Boo would no longer exist, the light would cease, and people would notice that the star hadn't existed for a long time. Some stars throbbed and sent out signals like some big lit-up broadcasting stations sailing across the sky. And all of space was rushing away at tremendous speed into some distance no one knew anything about. The farther into space one could see, the bigger it became. In the end, Grandpa had said, space would be so big that everything would be really close, except that no one would really notice that.

Mr. Boo tried to remember what Grandpa had meant by that. It would be fun to outfit a boat, take along a lot of tea, zwieback, and blankets, and sail out into that great dark sea of the air. Out there, a perennial wind blew: once it got started, there was nothing to stop it. Right now Grandpa and Pa and Ma might be sailing there, maybe they even shared a boat with a fire on the bottom to keep them warm, and with a lot of Grandpa's old books to read. Maybe there were many other boats as well, so there was no lack of company. It's possible if you can think of it, Mr. Boo thought.

Mr. Boo remembered Grandpa's beard and his brown coat with its powerful smell of tobacco. He felt lonesome. Outside, the woods rustled as the wind struck the dry tops of pinetrees. Some stray dog was digging for something in the back yard. The wind picked up, and Mr. Boo thought that he would only have to fix a sail on the chimney for the whole cottage to slowly rise into the air and run before the wind. He would hold the tiller and steer it along. Maybe he could ask Rimma and perhaps even that boy who'd been in his woodshed once, that Mikko. Maybe they, too, would like to go for a sail at night. Soon there would be a great big moon, the water of the air would be deep and clear like that of a wellspring. Then they could raise anchor and go.

Mr. Boo got up and poured himself a cup of tea, sipped and enjoyed it with his eyes closed. They would run into a planet, a star that received its light and heat from the sun just like Earth did, and they would land on it. Violets four hundred feet tall would rise up to the sun like stadium towers, and the butterflies would be the size of stone buildings. They themselves would be so tiny no one could see them or bother them. There, when you thought of a place, you instantly found yourself in that place. Or when you said "salt" you got a sugar cube. When you jumped into the water, you took off into the air. When you were asleep there, you were really awake. And no one could do anything bad there because it instantly changed into something good. No one does anything good to have it change into something bad, there's just no need for that. At least not until someone discovers that trick and starts using it.

Mr. Boo frowned. That sounded dangerous. Best not to think about it. Evil did not exist until someone invented it. From then on it had existed and gone on existing. Soon everybody wanted what others had, and when they acquired it one way or another, they didn't want it anymore now that everybody had it, and the competition went on and got worse. Only the Mr. Boos stayed away from it, Mr. Boo thought. I'm satisfied with what there is.

The floorboards creaked and some bird uttered a shrill cry outside. Soon it'll be morning, Mr. Boo thought, and I can go to sleep. Then there'll be another night, a new day, a new night. So it goes on, until one day you don't wake up anymore, you just go on sleeping. But you won't disappear altogether. Somewhere there is a new Mr. Boo, he may look a little different, but I'll go on through him, Mr. Boo thought. And once again there will be days and nights and days for him to live.

Mr. Boo rested his face in his hands and stared at the fire. Now its glow had darkened. Soon the embers would be black on top even though they still had a glowing heart inside. He felt tired. The lingonberry shrub on the windowsill nodded with its roots in the clear water like thick brown unraveled strands of wool.

Up above, space would go on humming and singing until the sun would rise and obscure its depth and turn the earth into a single blue sphere again. In the daytime you have to do your sailing in a real boat on a real lake. You have no business rising up into the air, certainly not with a flying cottage, Mr. Boo thought, and that may be just as well.

From high up in the air came the deep sound of an early jet plane, like thunder before a summer's rain. Mr. Boo gave a start and shook his head, then went and brushed his teeth carefully.

Mr. Boo Grows Some Flowers

One day Mr. Boo noticed that the birds in the trees were singing all the time. Small gray sparrows, yellow titmice, and bouncy starlings flew down to examine the dark soil, and the soil was steaming, and the trees pushed out leaves all over themselves. Even the wild vines showed a bit of green, and under the porch roof there were at least two bird's nests. At regular intervals the raucous cry of a pheasant was heard from the back yard. The air smelled clean and strong.

Mr. Boo thought things over and decided to do something, too. He rummaged in Grandpa's drawers and found a bag of seeds, got some soil from the yard, put it in a pot, placed the pot on a windowsill, dug the seeds into the soil and watered it. After a few days the first shoots showed up, and soon they started growing, racing each other along the windowframe. Mr. Boo tended them with an owner's pride.

Then it started raining. The rain fell like a dense gray veil and wiped everything clean, but when it went on and on, things began to get too damp. Wooden doors swelled up and windows warped so it was hard to close them anymore. The chimney didn't work properly, and the ceiling started leaking. Mr. Boo got a ladder and a nail, a piece of tarpaper and a hammer, and proceeded to fix the leak. He hit the nail as hard as he possibly could.

A horrendous yell of pain was heard in the room, followed by terrifying curses. Something awful had happened — Mr. Boos hardly ever use foul language.

"Except when they hit their thumbs with hammers," our unfortunate Mr. Boo hissed while wrapping his thumb with a thick bandage. Now he couldn't even think of fixing anything. Every time he moved his hand he felt a burning pain. So he dragged a wash basin under the leak and listened to the water dripping into the basin, monotonously and regularly.

This is better than the finest clock, Mr. Boo thought. All you need to do is count, and you know how much time has passed. He started counting. After reaching one thousand two hundred and thirty-eight Mr. Boo lost track. He didn't really know how much time had passed, he only knew that he had reached one thousand two hundred and thirty-eight.

Mr. Boo looked outside. It was getting dark. But now in the spring it got dark later. In any case, it's not night yet, Mr. Boo thought. That's all I need to know. And he turned and yawned noisily. But there was something that bothered him. Mr. Boo pondered what he had just seen. What he had seen had not been an ordinary window. He had seen a window that was green all over. Cautiously, Mr. Boo turned his head. Yes, this was true. The window and half the wall were covered by the green plant that grew in the pot, and from the plant hung small red blobs that looked just like little hands. These hands were by no means idle: they were busy cleaning and trimming leaves, discarding dead ones, working the soil. At that very moment one of the plant-hands moved at the speed of thought and caught a fly and quickly shoved it into something large and red that opened like a mouth. It was a mouth. Mr. Boo rubbed his eyes but the plant did not disappear, nor did its hands, and least of all its head. On the contrary — the head nodded to Mr. Boo when it noticed that he was watching it.

Mr. Boo sat stockstill. He couldn't have moved if he had wanted to. From where on earth had that terrifying plant appeared on his windowsill? Why had it chosen his windowsill — there were plenty of flowerpots and windowsills everywhere. But there it was and there it stayed. The plant nodded again, opened its mouth and said, in a very shrill but faint voice:

"I'm hungry."

Mr. Boo was horrified. He stared at the plant.

"I'm hungry," the plant said and waved impatiently with its many hands. "You don't have enough flies here. And you don't water me regularly, just whenever you happen to remember. I don't like that. I'm thirsty, too."

Without a word, Mr. Boo handed the plant a scoopful of water. It grabbed the scoop from his hand, tossed the water down and burped. Then it licked its lips and looked at Mr. Boo with an even more demanding expression.

"I'm hungry. Hurry up, give me something to eat."

"What kinds of things do you eat?" Mr. Boo asked. He was scared.

"What do I eat? Well, meat of course, but only good meat, I don't like bad meat at all. Raw beef is the best. But I'll take a frankfurter. Hold the relish, but give me a lot of ketchup and mustard."

Mr. Boo moved to the cupboard, mechanically like a toy train, and took down a can of cocktail sausages. The plant grabbed the can, opened a drawer, found the can opener, opened the can, and swallowed the sausages in less than thirty seconds. It didn't leave any for Mr. Boo, not that he had much of an appetite at that moment. He thought and thought, feverishly. Then he picked up his courage and asked:

"How did you get here?"

The plant looked surprised.

"Why, you planted me yourself, and then you took such good care of me — at first, that is. Now you're much lazier than you were then. But because you were so kind to me when I was little, I promise I won't devour you while you're asleep," said the plant and tried to look friendly. "That's a promise. I won't even do it when I'm terribly hungry and crave food."

You could have knocked Mr. Boo over with a matchstick, he was so appalled. It was Grandpa again. Never again will I touch anything of Grandpa's, Mr. Boo vowed to himself. I'll even learn to swim before I do that again. But how will I get rid of that thing? It'll grow and grow and need more food.

Soon it'll crowd me out of the house. And what if it gets so hungry one night that it forgets its promise and gobbles me up? I won't even know what hit me. No, nothing good will come of this.

"I'm thirsty," the plant said.

Mr. Boo handed the bucket to it. The plant drank it down making a lot of noise. Then it said:

"I need something to eat. I'm terribly hungry." The plant stretched out its hands and seemed to grow larger every second. The hands were moving along the ceiling and branching out in all directions. In a few days, those hands would be everywhere in the room, and then the plant would spread into the yard. First of all it would eat the nestling birds on the porch, then all the other birds. In a while, Mr. Boo thought with horror, not a single living creature would be left in the neighborhood. The more the plant ate, the bigger it would grow, and the more monstrous its appetite would be. It would start creeping toward the city where it would eat people, push its hands through open windows when people weren't watching, pull them out and devour them. I must prevent that, thought Mr. Boo and charged outside, slamming the door shut behind him. The plant shouted something but Mr. Boo didn't want to hear what it had to say.

In the woodshed Mr. Boo gathered up the axe and a pair of pliers and a couple of hammers and some nails. His thumb was still sore, but Mr. Boo ignored it. First he had to get rid of that plant. There would be time to think about his own aches and pains later. Mr. Boo snuck up to the window and peeked inside. The plant was just reaching into the pantry and taking out another can of food. When Mr. Boo rushed into the room the plant looked guilty. It put the can back into the pantry and said:

"I couldn't help it. I'm so hungry."

Then the plant grabbed the can again, opened it, and gulped down the contents. It took another can, opened it, and ate. And yet another. Now its conscience didn't bother it because Mr. Boo could see what it was doing. Soon, Mr. Boo realized, the plant would have eaten all the food in the cupboard.

In a blind rage, Mr. Boo rushed at the plant with his axe, ready to chop its stem — but the plant yanked the axe out of his hands without much effort and said, in a reproachful tone:

"I thought you were my friend. Don't do that again."

Mr. Boo got mad. This was too much. He threw the pliers at the plant as hard as he could. But the pliers bounced back off the plant's stem and almost hit Mr. Boo in the eye.

It's like rubber, Mr. Boo thought in despair. I can't do anything to it.

The plant smiled a cunning smile. Then it flicked Mr. Boo's nose with one of its hands and said:

"Food. And don't try any tricks ..." Its hand made a warning gesture.

"All right, all right," Mr. Boo stammered.

"No tricks! You understand? Get me some meat, and pronto!"

"All right, all right," said Mr. Boo, and when the plant let him go, he mustered all his strength and ran to the door. The plant tried to grab him but only got hold of his sleeve, and since Mr. Boo's coat was old, the sleeve came off and remained in the plant's hand. Mr. Boo managed to scramble outside and bar the door behind himself.

He stopped in the yard, panting. This was the worst of it: he would be the plant's slave for the rest of his life. I just can't think of what to do, Mr. Boo thought. His thoughts were bouncing around like rabbits in a cage. Who could help me? The beaver was gone. The children were too small, the plant would eat them. I can't ask them to help me. Grown-ups won't have anything to do with me. Oh, never again will I enjoy my peaceful home and sip my tea! Mr. Boo was crying. Big tears ran down his cheeks.

"Why are you crying?" Mikko asked. He had snuck up from the direction of the apple tree, wanting to scare Mr. Boo, but then deciding against it because Mr. Boo looked so miserable.

"Is there anything I can do to help?"

Mr. Boo cried and shook his head. Then he tried to regain his dignity. That kid will never again be scared of me if he sees me weeping, he thought. He swallowed and said:

"I'm all right."

"No one cries for no reason," said Mikko.

"I do. Besides, I wasn't crying. I was laughing."

"Oh, I thought ..." and Mikko stopped in mid-sentence because he realized that Mr. Boo was embarrassed to have been caught crying.

"Well, yes, I see. It was raining here, wasn't it?"

"So it was," Mr. Boo said cheerfully. "So it was."

"But even clouds have a reason for raining, don't they?"

"Clouds rain when they're being persecuted by carnivorous plants."

"Carnivorous plants?"

"That's right. In there." Mr. Boo pointed at his cottage. "It eats every bit of meat it sees, and it keeps growing all the time. No one can do anything about it. It's like rubber. I tried. Now I have to get some more meat for it. Or else it'll eat me."

Mikko listened in silence and understood right away that this was a serious matter.

"Why don't you move away?" he asked.

"I have no place else to go. And if I leave, it'll eat all the birds," Mr. Boo said and swallowed hard.

"So sharp weapons won't work on it?" Mikko asked.

"No. I tried."

Mikko thought for a moment. Then his eyes brightened.

"Let's put it to sleep," he suggested.

"How can we do that?" Mr. Boo asked, sounding quite discouraged.

"Wait here a minute."

Mikko started running to his house. Mr. Boo waited and waited. At last Mikko returned, panting. He had a big sausage in one hand and a can in the other. The side of the can had pictures of flowers on it.

"Try this," Mikko panted.

Surprised, Mr. Boo stared at the jar.

"What is it?"

"It's deodorant. Like a sweat remover," Mikko said. "I thought it might help. You could at least try. I can't think of anything else. Look, when you push here, it sprays."

Mr. Boo was appalled.

"Put that thing away, immediately. It might be dangerous."

Mikko reassured him. "Take it easy. I'd never push the spray button. This thing belongs to my mother and she's told me not to fool with it. But you could at least try. It might scare the plant. And I won't ever mess with it again."

Mr. Boo took the deodorant spray can. In the face of real danger he had to act without delay. He concealed the can under his coat, took the sausage, looked at Mikko with a silent plea in his eyes, and slowly walked back to the door. Mikko followed him on tiptoe.

The plant had grown some more. It was very angry and very hungry. It felt that it had had to wait far too long. The plant bopped Mr. Boo in the nose with one of its hands and jerked the sausage out of his hand with another. It swallowed the sausage incredibly fast, then cast a demanding glance at Mr. Boo. The plant was so hungry that it would have eaten small rocks if there had been any nearby. But there was, of course, Mr. Boo. The plant forgot its promise and grabbed Mr. Boo by the collar. Mr. Boo whipped out his spray can and sprayed the plant, but the only result of that was a fragrance of flowers that spread through the room. The plant's hands grabbed Mr. Boo everywhere.

"Mikko, help!" Mr. Boo shouted, and Mikko rushed in immediately.

Mikko was holding a rock with sharp edges and he threw it with all his might at the plant's head. Since all of the plant's hands were busy holding down Mr. Boo, it didn't have time to catch the rock. The plant opened its mouth, and the rock zoomed into it with the same ease soccer balls end up in the Finland team's goal. The plant swallowed once. It didn't say anything. But now the deodorant did begin to take effect. The plant's hands loosened their grip, its eyes closed slowly, and Mr. Boo managed to free himself.

Shakily, Mr. Boo got to his feet. What now? The danger was by no means a thing of the past. The plant probably wouldn't remain unconscious for very long. And when it woke up ... Mr. Boo didn't even want to imagine what would happen then. The plant would be beside itself with rage.

Then he remembered something!

"Quick," Mr. Boo shouted to Mikko and ran to the closet. He pulled out a small blue glass pearl with a tiny silver stopper. Then he turned to Mikko:

"Promise you won't ever tell anyone what will happen now."

Mikko promised.

Quickly Mr. Boo ran over to the plant and took the stopper out of the pearl. He tilted the pearl, and a small pale yellow drop of liquid fell onto the plant's stem. That very instant, the whole plant disappeared without a sound. It simply wasn't there anymore. No trace of it remained, not even a small puddle of milk, as after the huge cat. The plant was gone, and that was that.

Mikko stared, looking as surprised as a person could ever be.

"How did you do that?" he whispered.

Mr. Boo turned to Mikko, still trembling and as white as a piece of chalk.

"Hush, don't say anything about it anymore. This was just a bad dream. Remember: you promised."

Mikko nodded. It was quiet. They could hear the birds sing in the trees in the yard. In the woods, a dog barked and another one joined in. A cat ran like a shadow across the garden.

Mr. Boo sat down on a chair and stared straight ahead. He was utterly exhausted. Mikko nudged him.

"Hey, listen — may I come back and visit some time?"

Mr. Boo smiled. Very, very slowly he managed to say:

"Sure. Come whenever you like."

And then Mr. Boo was fast asleep. The room was filled with his slow heavy breathing. Mr. Boo slept and slept.

Mikko waited a while, then left. It was a warm spring day. The gravel roads were drying out. Mikko ran down the road faster than anyone else in the world. Then he slowed down and walked in the ditch, trying to get his gym shoes wet. He thought about Mr. Boo. That little old guy was a real magician.

I have to go see him again sometime. Next time I go, I bet he'll have five lions and a family of ostriches there. I must ask him some time how he really does those tricks. Maybe he'll teach me!

And Mikko ran again for a good while. No one in the whole world would be a match for him! He'd show them all!

Hannu Mäkelä (1943-) is one of contemporary Finland's most beloved authors of children's books. His *Mr. Boo (Herra Huu)* series, illustrated by the author, became a classic favorite immediately when it first appeared in 1973. The other parts of the series are entitled *Herra Huu saa naapurin* (1974) (*Mr. Boo Gets a Neighbor*) and *Herra Huu muuttaa* (1975) (*Mr. Boo Moves*). Mäkelä has authored several other children's books for young people of all ages.

Hannu Mäkelä's novels and poetry for adults have earned him a reputation as one of Finland's most accomplished authors. He was awarded the coveted Finlandia Prize in Literature in 1995 for his novel *Mestari* (*The Master*) about the life of Eino Leino (1867-1926), Finland's celebrated poet and playwright. Mäkelä has edited and compiled dozens of collections of stories and poetry. Hannu Mäkelä's works have been translated to several languages. Mr. Boo is his first book in English translation.